13
X

JACK THE RIPPER

JACK THE RIPPER

Murder, Mystery and Intrigue
in London's East End

HISTORY/CRIME

by Susan McNicoll

For Polly Nichols, Annie Chapman, Elizabeth Stride,
Catherine Eddowes and Mary Jane Kelly

PUBLISHED BY ALTITUDE PUBLISHING CANADA LTD.
1500 Railway Avenue, Canmore, Alberta T1W 1P6
www.altitudepublishing.com
1-800-957-6888

Extreme care has been taken to ensure that all information presented in
this book is accurate and up to date. Neither the author nor the
publisher can be held responsible for any errors.

Publisher	Stephen Hutchings
Associate Publisher	Kara Turner
Series Editor	Jill Foran
Editor	Georgina Montgomery
Digital Photo Colouring	Bryan Pezzi

We acknowledge the financial support of the Government
of Canada through the Book Publishing Industry Development
Program (BPIDP) for our publishing activities.

Altitude GreenTree Program
Altitude Publishing will plant twice as many trees as were used
in the manufacturing of this product.

We acknowledge the support of the Canada Council for the Arts which
in 2003 invested $21.7 million in writing and publishing throughout Canada.

Canada Council   Conseil des Arts
for the Arts   du Canada

National Library of Canada Cataloguing in Publication Data

McNicoll, Susan
Jack the Ripper / Susan McNicoll.

(Amazing stories)
Includes bibliographical references.
ISBN 1-55265-900-3

1. Jack, the Ripper. 2. Serial murders--England--London--
History--19th century. 3. Whitechapel (London, England)--History.
I. Title. II. Series: Amazing stories (Canmore, Alta.)

HV6535.G6L65 2005   364.152'3'092   C2005-900946-2

An application for the trademark for Amazing Stories™
has been made and the registered trademark is pending.

Printed and bound in Canada by Friesens
2 4 6 8 9 7 5 3 1

Contents

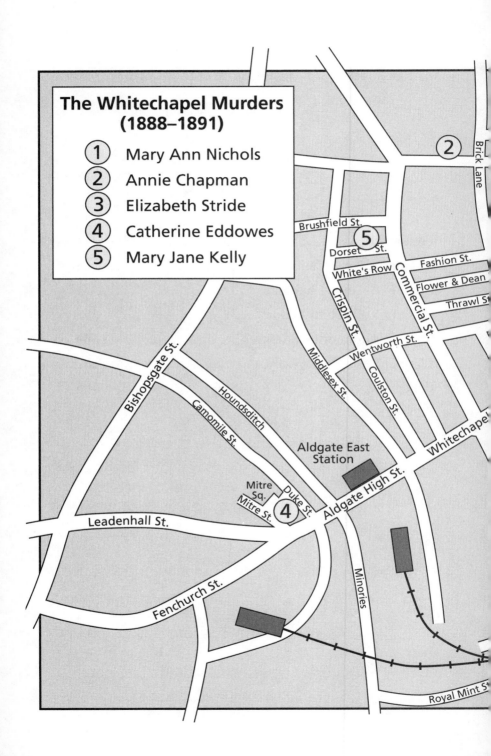

The Whitechapel Murders (1888–1891)

1. Mary Ann Nichols
2. Annie Chapman
3. Elizabeth Stride
4. Catherine Eddowes
5. Mary Jane Kelly

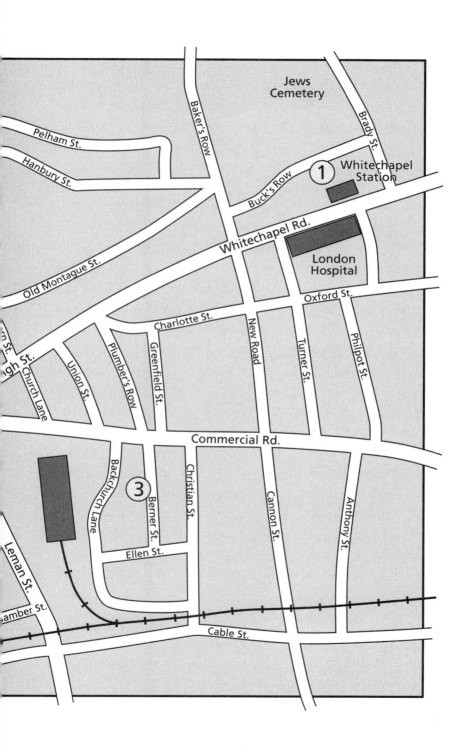

Prologue

Officially, she would be the first.

As Polly went off in search of the fourpence needed for lodgings that night, the 42-year-old was about to go down in history. Three times during the day she had had enough money to sleep safe that night – and three times Polly drank it away.

One of the coldest and wettest summers on record was coming to a close in 1888. A thunderstorm earlier in the evening and continuing sporadic showers had left the cobblestone road very slippery. It was after 3.15 in the morning as she drunkenly staggered along Buck's Row in London's gritty East End.

Polly was one of the "unfortunates", as Victorians called the women who, for one reason or another, had turned to prostitution to survive.

The section of the road she walked along was narrow, with shabby, two-storey houses lining one side and high warehouse walls lining the other. The only light came from a single gas street lamp which, from the end of the road, cast long, eerie shadows on the cobblestones and left the pavement in virtual darkness.

Hearing someone behind her in the street, Polly turned and saw a man in the distance. She paused to steady herself

*against a closed gateway. Hoping to offer her services and col-
lect the money needed for the night's lodgings, she smoothed
out her skirts and straightened her bonnet.*

*Polly turned to face the man and started to say hello,
but the word never left her lips. Clamping one hand over her
mouth, he shoved her to the ground so viciously that her teeth
cut into her tongue. With his other hand he gripped her throat,
strangling her until she lost consciousness.*

*Then, with a long-bladed knife, the man sliced a 4-inch
cut across Polly's neck, followed by another longer swipe below
it from left ear to right.*

Jack the Ripper was born.

Chapter 1
Polly Nichols

She lived hard and drank hard, but Mary Ann Nichols still looked considerably younger than her 42 years. She had brown eyes, brown hair just starting to grey and high cheekbones under a dark complexion. A number of her front teeth were missing and a childhood scar was still visible on her forehead. She was only 5 feet, 2 inches tall and on the plump side.

Born to Edward and Caroline Walker in 1845, Mary Ann (known to everyone as Polly) married machinist William Nichols in 1864. Between then and 1879, Polly gave birth to five children. The couple separated four or five times through the years over Polly's drinking and she walked out for the last time in 1881. Her father said the marriage ended because William had had an affair with the nurse who cared for Polly "during her last confinement [pregnancy]". William said the affair did not happen until long after his wife left him. Regardless of why Polly left him and her four youngest children, William still gave her five shillings a week to live on. Their oldest child, a boy, had gone to live with Polly's father and was reportedly estranged from his father at the time of his mother's death.

In 1882, when William found out his wife was living as a prostitute, he discontinued his support payments to her. Parish authorities tried to collect maintenance money from him, but he was able to win his case by proving Polly had deserted him and the children and turned to prostitution.

Whatever the truth was, there was no doubt that alcohol was Polly's nemesis and would end up robbing her of everything, even her life.

* * *

Charles Cross left his home in Bethnal Green at 3.30 a.m. on Friday, 31 August 1888 and headed to work. He walked along Buck's Row in the Whitechapel District of London's East End. The rough cobblestone street ran parallel to Whitechapel Road just behind the Underground station that had only been open for four years. Buck's Row was bounded on one end by Brady Street and the other by Baker's Row. The one gas lamp at the end of the street cast very little light, but Cross thought he saw something lying up against a gateway on the opposite side of the road. He later stated he thought it was a tarpaulin, but when he stepped into the road to take a closer look he realised it was the body of a woman. One hand was resting against the gateway and the other near a black bonnet close by her head. Her clothes were pulled up to the top of her thighs. At first Cross thought maybe she had been raped and "was still in a swoon" over it. He was wrong.

He heard another man, John Paul, who was on his way to work in Spitalfields.

"Come and look over here," Cross called out to him. "There's a woman."

The two of them knelt down and Cross took hold of her clenched fist. It was cold.

"I believe she's dead," he said.

Paul wasn't as sure. He touched her face and it was warm. Putting his hand over her heart, he told Cross, "I think she is breathing, but it is very little if she is." He wanted Cross to help him sit her up, but Cross wanted no part of it.

"I am not going to touch her," he replied.

It was a very dark night or the two men would have had no doubts about how very dead the woman was. They were now both late, so Paul tried, unsuccessfully, to pull her clothes down before the two men decided to head to work and tell the first policeman they saw.

They found Police Constable G. Mizen and told him of the woman in Buck's Row. Cross later testified he told Constable Mizen the woman "was either dead or drunk" and that Paul added "I think she's dead". Mizen apparently replied,

"All right", but then took his time heading to Buck's Row.

* * *

Police Constable John Neil had walked along Buck's Row at 3.15 a.m. and found nothing amiss. On his next rounds a half hour later, he noticed a figure lying partly in the street.

"I went across and found [the] deceased lying outside a gateway, her head towards the east," Neil testified at the inquest. "The gateway was closed. It was about nine or ten feet high and led to some stables … Deceased was lying lengthways along the street, her left hand touching the gate. I examined the body by the aid of my lantern, and noticed blood oozing from a wound in the throat.

"She was lying on her back, with her clothes disarranged. I felt her arm, which was quite warm from the joints upwards. Her eyes were wide open. Her bonnet was off and lying at her side, close to the left hand."

Another officer, Police Constable John Thain, had also passed by the end of Buck's Row at 3.15 a.m. and found it quiet. Passing by again at 3.45, he saw a lamp signal from Constable Neil and found him standing beside the body.

"In the gutter there was a large quantity of blood which had run off the pavement," Thain reported. "The deceased's clothing was saturated with blood, which appeared to have run from her back."

"For God's sake, Jack! Go and fetch the doctor!" Neil

commanded. Constable Mizen also appeared at this time after having met up with Cross and Paul. Neil sent him for an ambulance. Most ambulances at this time were used by the police. They were wooden-sided handcarts with a black leather bottom and straps to tie the patient down.

Before the doctor arrived, Constable Neil rang the doorbell of Essex Wharf, directly opposite from where the body lay. A local resident told the constable that his wife was awake the whole night and that it had been unusually quiet.

"If the woman had called out", the man said, "or had been quarrelling with anybody ... [we] would have been sure to hear the noise."

Neil returned to the woman and examined the ground around her body.

"Knowing that the body was warm, did it not strike you that it might just have been laid there, and that the woman was killed elsewhere?" Constable Neil was asked at the inquest.

He replied that he'd examined the road for wheel marks but found none. Numerous other people residing in Buck's Row also swore there had been no noise, no sound of anyone calling out. Whitechapel Road was a busy thoroughfare in the early morning, Neil told the inquest, and anyone could have escaped along it without attracting attention.

Dr Rees Ralph Llewellyn lived nearby on Whitechapel Road and was at the scene by 4.00 a.m.

"I found she ... had severe injuries to the throat," Llewellyn later testified. "Her hands and wrists were cold, but the body and lower extremities were warm. I examined her chest and felt her heart."

"It was dark at the time," he added, perhaps trying to explain how he missed the victim's worst wound of all – severe injuries to the abdomen. He estimated she had not been dead more than half an hour.

The body was lifted onto the ambulance and taken to the nearby Whitechapel Workhouse mortuary. When Inspector John Spratling arrived at the mortuary, the body still lay on the ambulance out in the yard. While waiting for the "keeper of the dead-house" to arrive with the keys, Spratling took down a description of the deceased but did not closely examine her body. It was only once inside when he began to remove her clothes to begin his examination that he found the victim had been disembowelled. Dr Llewellyn was immediately summoned.

His post-mortem examination showed:

- a laceration to the tongue;
- on the right side of the face, running along the lower part of the jaw, a bruise that might have been caused by a blow with the fist or pressure from fingers;
- a circular bruise on the left side of the face that also might have been caused by pressure of the fingers;
- on the left side of the neck, about an inch below the jaw, an incision about 4 inches long

and running vertically from a point immediately below the ear;

- about an inch below and ahead of the first incision, a second incision running circularly to a point 3 inches below the right jaw (this incision, about 8 inches long, completely severed all the tissues down to the vertebrae and the large vessels of the neck);
- about 2 to 3 inches from the left side of the lower abdomen, a very deep wound that cut jaggedly through the tissues;
- several smaller incisions that ran across the abdomen; and
- on the right side of the abdomen, three or four similar cuts, running downwards.

All the injuries, Dr Llewellyn said, were inflicted by the same instrument, a sharp, long-bladed knife, and done "with great violence" in a downward motion. Because the injuries occurred from left to right, Llewellyn initially felt the killer was likely left-handed (though later he came to doubt his own conclusions about that and about the knife having a long blade). There was no evidence of rape, or "sexual connexion" as the Victorians called it.

The police found on the body the only earthly possessions Polly Nichols owned: a white handkerchief, a comb and a piece of broken mirror.

An examination of the clothes did not help in the determination of how the wounds were inflicted. The clothes had been cut off by two inmates of the mortuary as they were preparing the body for the doctor and they had no idea they were destroying vital evidence. There were many layers of clothing and they were difficult to pry off the body, they told the inquest.

The victim had been wearing all the clothes she owned: a black straw bonnet trimmed with black velvet, a reddish-brown Ulster overcoat with seven large brass buttons, a new brown linsey frock, a white flannel chest cloth, black ribbed wool stockings, two petticoats, brown stays, flannel drawers and a pair of men's elastic-sided boots.

Inspector Spratling, in describing the clothing, said the two petticoats had the marks of the Lambeth Workhouse, Princes Road, on them. Inspector Joseph Helson of the Criminal Investigation Department cut out these marks in the hope they would help to identify the victim. They did.

On the evening of 31 August, Mary Ann Monk, an inmate at Lambeth Workhouse, tentatively identified the victim as Mary Ann (Polly) Nichols, whom she had met some months earlier at the workhouse. The following afternoon, William Nichols went to the mortuary with one of his sons and positively identified his wife. It was reported that he was greatly upset at the sight of her.

"I forgive you, as you are, for what you have been to me," the newspapers reported him saying.

Polly Nichols

* * *

The newspapers, in fact, were to play a major role in the phenomenon that became Jack the Ripper. The Education Act of 1870 had brought about improved educational standards, the result of which was increased literacy. This, along with the removal of taxes on advertising and then on newspapers themselves in 1885, combined to create a boom in the newspaper business, especially the "penny dailies". By the time Jack the Ripper hit the scene in 1888, Britain had 180 dailies. The battles for circulation coincided with the start of this series of murders – murders whose abhorrence was shocking even by East End standards.

People with nowhere else to go lived in the East End, if you could call what they did living. It included the London docks and the areas of Whitechapel, Spitalfields and Bethnal Green. In 1888, there were approximately a million people crammed into grim slums. If they could afford one, they lived in a room furnished with a bed, table and chair, but more often they stayed in a common lodging house, spending fourpence a night to share a bed. It was estimated that in 1888 there were 233 such lodging houses in Whitechapel alone. There were also 62 brothels and a reported 1200 prostitutes. This was a conservative estimate, for many of the local women resorted to casual prostitution at one time or another.

The price for a prostitute of Polly's low standing could be as little as twopence. The price of a large glass of gin was threepence.

And for those without even the fourpence to spend on a bed, there were the workhouses. Some preferred to die rather than enter them.

"Poverty, misery and fear of the workhouse are the principal causes of suicide among the working classes," Jack London wrote in 1902 in *The People of the Abyss*, his book about the degradations he witnessed in the slums of East London. London had undertaken to do a personal social study, to see for himself what life was like in the East End. He painted a sad and desperate picture.

"'I'll drown myself before I go into the workhouse,' said Ellen Hughes Hunt, aged fifty-two," wrote London. "Last Wednesday they held an inquest on her body ... her husband came from the Islington Workhouse to testify. He had been a cheesemonger but failure in business and poverty had driven him into the workhouse, whither his wife had refused to accompany him. She was last seen at one in the morning. Three hours later her hat and jacket were found on the towing path by the Regent's Canal, and later her body was fished from the water. Verdict: suicide during temporary insanity.

"[I]t is as fair and logical to say that her husband was suffering from temporary insanity when he went into the Islington Workhouse as ... when she went into the Regent's Canal," London continued. "... I for one, from what I know of canals and workhouses, should choose the canal, were I in a similar position."

London's friends thought him mad taking up this investigation, and even the driver of his cab took considerable persuading before starting the horse in the direction of the East End.

"The region my hansom was now penetrating was one unending slum," wrote London. "The streets were filled with a new and different race of people, short of stature, and of wretched or beer-sodden appearance. We rolled along through miles of bricks and squalor, and from each cross street and alley flashed long vistas of bricks and misery. Here and there lurched a drunken man or woman, and the air was obscene with sounds of jangling and squabbling.

"At a market, tottery old men and women were searching in the garbage thrown in the mud for rotten potatoes, beans, and vegetables, while little children clustered like flies around a festering mass of fruit, thrusting their arms to the shoulders into the liquid corruption, and drawing forth morsels, but partially decayed, which they devoured on the spot ... [F]or the first time in my life the fear of the crowd smote me."

Union workhouses were home to many of those at the lowest end of society's spectrum and had been since the 1600s. Set up by church parishes, their main purpose was relief of destitution. They were never used as a form of punishment. The Poor Law Amendment Act of 1834 changed that, limiting workhouse admittance to the deserving poor rather than the undeserving poor. The idea was to make conditions in workhouses so difficult that only those desperate enough would want to enter them. Able-bodied men and women, it was thought, would rush to find a job rather than endure the workhouse.

It didn't work. People ended up in workhouses because they were usually too poor, too old, or too ill to support themselves. For unmarried pregnant women who were disowned by their families, the workhouses were the only option.

In spite of the horrible conditions, workhouses were often full and there were not enough spaces for those wanting to get in. Queues started forming at 1.00 p.m. for the few beds that would become free for the night. People were searched before entry and if they had any money on them at all, they were not admitted. If you were accepted for the night, you had to stay through the next day and work in one of many unpleasant jobs. If you wanted to leave, you had to give the administration three hours' notice. And still the admitting queues continued. Jack London wrote that it took him three tries before he was even able to enter one. On entering, he had what he thought was a brick thrust into his hands.

"I looked at the brick in my hand, and saw that by doing violence to the language it might be called 'bread'," he wrote. "The light was very dim down in the cellar, and before I knew it some other man had thrust a pannikin [small drinking vessel] into my other hand. Then I stumbled on to a still darker room, where were benches and tables and men ... [M]ost of the men were suffering from tired feet, and they prefaced the meal by removing their shoes and unbinding the filthy rags with which their feet were wrapped." The pannikin contained three-quarters of a pint of skilly, a mixture of hot water and Indian corn.

"The men were dipping their bread into heaps of salt scattered over the dirty tables," London wrote. "I attempted the same, but the bread seemed to stick in my mouth."

His night became even worse when he awoke towards morning with a rat on his chest. London only made it through half a day of repulsive and dangerous work at the workhouse infirmary before he had enough and bolted over the fence to freedom.

* * *

The Renfrew Road site of the Lambeth Workhouse opened in 1884 and was a traditional workhouse with able and disabled inmates. Polly Nichols spent some months there early in 1883 before she moved in with her father later in the same year.

That arrangement only lasted for two months. "Well, at times she drank and that was why we did not agree," he said at the inquest into her death. He also said that Polly voluntarily moved out of his house and back into Lambeth Workhouse.

In June 1883 she began a four-year relationship with a blacksmith named Thomas Dew. It appeared to be a stable period in her life. In 1886, while she was living with Dew,

Polly attended the funeral of her brother who had been killed in an accident. Her family said she had been respectably dressed at the time. It is not known why her relationship with Dew ended, but when it did, Polly's name again turned up on workhouse records in October 1887. That December she was caught by police "sleeping rough" in Trafalgar Square. Found to be destitute, she was sent once again to the Lambeth Workhouse, although this time it was the Princes Road site.

The Lambeth Workhouse on Princes Road was established in 1887 as a test workhouse for 200 men and 150 women. It was in this workhouse that Polly Nichols spent many months of her final year. Men and women were segregated into three classes in the workhouse, according to their previous conduct. Men typically did the harder physical work such as breaking stones into smaller pieces for use in building roads. Women mostly did cleaning, cooking, spinning and weaving. They also did a great deal of "oakum picking" – picking fibre out of the middle of rope, which was then mixed with tar and used as caulking in wooden ships. The days in the workhouse were long and regimented, beginning at 6.00 a.m. and ending with bed at 8.00 p.m.

Sometimes workhouses arranged outside domestic positions for female residents. This was the case for Polly who, in May 1888, took a position as a domestic servant for Samuel and Sarah Cowdry. It seemed to be an attempt by Polly to make a better life for herself, and for a time she seemed happy. In a letter to her father, she wrote:

I just right [sic] to say you will be glad to know that I am settled in my new place, and going all right up to now. My people went out yesterday and have not returned, so I am left in charge. It is a grand place inside, with trees and gardens back and front. All has been newly done up. They are teetotallers and religious so I ought to get on. They are very nice people, and I have not too much to do. I hope you are all right and the boy has work. So good bye for the present. From yours truly, Polly.

Apparently, however, Polly could not handle good fortune. Two months into her new job she stole clothing worth £3 10 shillings and left. Having had enough of workhouses, she moved into a common lodging house on Thrawl Street, where she shared a room with four women, including one named Emily Holland.

A week before her murder, Polly moved once more, this time to a lodging house known as the White House on Flower and Dean Street. In this place men were allowed to share a bed with a woman, which was most likely why Polly chose it. Many of the common lodging houses catered to prostitutes. (Five years prior to Polly's murder, Flower and Dean Street was described in a London newspaper as "perhaps the foulest and most dangerous street in the whole metropolis".)

Late on the evening of 30 August 1888, Polly was seen walking down Whitechapel Road. At 12.30 a.m. she left the

Frying Pan public house and made her way to a lodging house on Thrawl Street. An hour later she was asked to leave because she could not produce the fourpence required.

"Never mind. I'll soon get my doss [bed] money. See what a jolly bonnet I've got now," she said, pointing to a little black bonnet no one had seen Polly wearing before.

It was about 2.30 a.m. and Emily Holland was returning from watching the Shadwell Dry Dock fire that had lit up the sky over part of London that same evening. She met Polly at the corner of Whitechapel Road and Osborn Street. Polly was "very drunk and staggered against the wall," Emily told the inquest, adding that Polly said she had drunk her doss money away three times that day.

"After one more attempt to find trade, she would return to Flower and Dean Street where she could share a bed with a man," Emily said.

Although Emily tried to persuade her to return to the Thrawl Street lodging house with her instead, Polly walked off down Whitechapel Road and into the arms of a killer.

The inquest lasted for four days over three weeks, but did not lead to any ideas as to the murderer's identity. Most of the inquest focused on tracking Polly's activities leading up to the murder. It was pointed out many times that no sounds were heard by any witnesses during the night and early hours when she was killed. Self-confessed light sleeper Emma Green slept through the assault even though her window was less than three feet from the spot where Polly died.

Polly Nichols

Although she was the first official victim of the man who would come to be known as Jack the Ripper, Polly was the third woman to be murdered within a short space of time and early theories believed them all to be the work of one man. There are still some Ripperologists (people who continue to study the crimes) who believe one of the earlier victims, Martha Tambram, was Jack the Ripper's first victim.

Outrage was growing at the seeming inability of the police to find out who was responsible. Even in the squalor of the East End, the murders were taking on a life of their own, fuelled by the never-ending press coverage. Many papers called for officials to offer a reward and the refusal by them to do this increased police criticism. Local residents were putting together a reward but, officially, none was forthcoming. The foreman of the jury at the inquest said the government should be offering a "substantial reward".

"If it had been a rich person that was murdered there would have been a reward of £1,000 offered", he said, "but as it was a poor unfortunate hardly any notice was taken."

The coroner was not happy.

"I think you are wrong altogether, and have no right to make such statements," he replied. "For some time past the offering of rewards has been discontinued, no distinction being made between rich and poor."

"Nevertheless", the foreman said, "I maintain that if a large reward had been offered in the George Yard murder [of Martha Tambram] the last horrible murder would not have been committed. I am glad to see inhabitants are themselves going to offer a reward, and I will myself give £25."

In the week following the murder, in spite of talking to every resident on Buck's Row, the police gave out few details. The only statement regarding suspects was brief. "Whatever information may be in possession of the police they deem it necessary to keep secret, but ... it is believed that their attention is particularly directed to two individuals, one a notorious character known as 'Leather Apron', and the other a seafaring man," the *Manchester Guardian* reported.

Buck's Row, where it all started, became synonymous with evil and was dubbed "Killer's Row". Eventually it became too much for the residents of the street and they petitioned for a name change. In 1892, Buck's Row and its extension, White's Row, joined to become Durward Street.

On Thursday, 6 September 1888, Polly was buried at the City of London Cemetery at Manor Park in public grave #210752. Expenses for the funeral were paid for by her father, estranged husband and son Edward Nichols. The polished elm coffin carrying Polly's remains was taken from the mortuary to an undertaker on Hanbury Street. As the cortège left from there for the cemetery and drove along Hanbury Street, they could not possibly know that this road would be the location of the next brutal murder little more than a day later.

Chapter 2
Annie Chapman

Oh Dark Annie,
what made you turn on Hanbury Street that eve
were you cold, was business slow
had your men all taken leave

from the song "Dark Annie", written by
Annie's descendent, Aaron Chapman

I n many ways, the residents of 29 Hanbury Street in September 1888 were a perfect cross-section of those living in East End houses, where furnished rooms were often rented out on a long-term basis. They were hard working, even industrious. In the early 21st century, some of them might even have been called entrepreneurs, but in the 1880s they were simply poor and doing their best to survive, carving out a little niche by offering services or products to others in the area.

Their residence was built, like hundreds of others, for

the Spitalfield weavers. When hand looms were replaced by steam and power, these buildings were converted to housing for the poor. The dingy three-storey house at No. 29 was on the north side of the street, flanked by two other equally dilapidated structures. The eight-room house had two front doors. One led into a shop. Over the other, on the left, a sign read "Mrs A. Richardson, rough packing-case maker". It opened into a 23-foot-long passageway. A staircase led to the upper rooms, while the ground level corridor continued through to a door that opened onto the small backyard where the lavatory and a wood shed were. From the yard, a cellar door led down to Mrs Richardson's workshop. A five-foot-high wooden fence separated the yard from the adjoining neighbours and the only way to leave the yard was back through the house. Some of the tenants left for work very early in the morning, some as early as 1.00 a.m., so it was the practice to leave both front and back doors of the house unlocked.

Amelia Richardson did not own the house, but rented a large portion of it, subletting to others. She occupied the ground and first floors and workshops in the cellar.

"I carry on the business of a packing-case maker there," she later said, adding that the cellar and the backyard were both used in the manufacturing process.

She and her grandson slept in a first-floor room, facing the street. Also on this floor were Mr Walker, who was "a maker of lawn-tennis boots", and his mildly retarded son.

The ground floor's front room was occupied by Mrs Harriet Hardiman and her 16-year-old son. They slept there and operated a cat's meat shop out of it (cat's meat being food for cats and dogs). The other ground floor room was used by Amelia Richardson for cooking and for her weekly prayer meetings. The back room of the second floor was occupied by two unmarried sisters who worked in a cigar factory. The front room was occupied by Mr Thompson, his wife, and his adopted daughter. He was a carman, a person who drove cart horses to deliver sellers' products to their customers.

The rear attic room was occupied by Sarah Cox, an elderly woman who Richardson kept "out of charity." John Davis lived with his wife and three sons in the other room at the top of the house, the newest tenants of 29 Hanbury Street that September, having only been there a month. Davis was a porter at Leadenhall Market.

Saturday, 8 September 1888 was market day. Davis's sleep had been restless and he lay awake from 3.00 to 5.00 a.m. that morning before falling back to sleep. When he awoke again, the Spitalfields Church clock was striking 5.45 a.m.

Thompson, the carman, had already left for work at 3.50 a.m. Mrs Richardson, as she was later to testify, heard him leave and called out "good morning." She swore she heard no one else that night. Her son, John, worked for her business but did not live on the premises. He also worked at the market on Saturdays and, because of a recent break-in of the cellar, stopped by between 4.45 and 4.50 a.m. to check the security of the cellar door.

"The yard door was shut," John would later recall. "I opened it and sat on the doorstep and cut a piece of leather off my boot with an old table-knife."

The sky was beginning to lighten and he noticed nothing amiss. He could see the padlock on the cellar was secure and he left. The door closed automatically behind him.

John Davis had a cup of tea with his wife and went downstairs to the backyard to use the lavatory.

"Neither of the doors [front or back] was able to be locked", he later stated, "and I have never seen them locked. Anyone who knows where the latch of the front door is could open it and go along the passage into the yard. It is a large yard. Facing the door, on the opposite side, on my left as I was standing, there is a shed where Mrs Richardson keeps her wood. In the right-hand corner there is a closet [lavatory]."

As soon as he opened the back door, Davis saw the woman. She was lying to his left, head towards the house and legs towards the wood shed. Seeing blood and that her clothes "were up to her groins", he dashed back along the corridor and out into the street looking for help. James Green and James Kent were standing outside their workshop a few doors away when they saw Davis running towards them shouting, "Men, come here!" Henry John Holland was on his way to work and joined the men as they returned to the house.

"I could see the woman was dead," Kent later stated. "The face and hands were besmeared with blood, as if she had struggled. She appeared to have been on her back and fought with her hands to free herself. The hands were turned towards her throat."

They went off in search of the police. Kent was particularly shaken and when he couldn't locate a policeman right away, he returned to his workshop and took some brandy to steady his nerves. He then found a piece of canvas to cover the body and returned to the house. By this time Inspector Chandler had arrived to take possession of the yard and the remains of who would turn out to be Annie Chapman, or "Dark Annie" as she was known.

She was 47 years old and what had been done to her body would horrify a nation and the world.

Little is known about Annie Chapman's early life except that she was born Eliza Anne Smith in September 1841, six months before her parents' marriage. On 1 May 1869, Annie married John Chapman, a coachman, and they lived with her mother. They were in their own home by 1870, and in 1881 they moved to Windsor, where John took a job as a domestic coachman. They had three children: Emily Ruth (born 1870), Annie Georgina (born 1873) and John (born 1881). Young John was born crippled and sent to a home. Emily Ruth died of meningitis at the age of 12.

Whether these losses were contributing factors is not known, but the couple separated by mutual consent in 1884 or 1885. Police reports said it was because of Annie's "drunken and immoral ways". While it is true that she was arrested many times in Windsor for drunkenness, her husband was also a heavy drinker and died on Christmas Day, 1886, from cirrhosis of the liver.

Until his death, John paid Annie 10 shillings a week by Post Office order. Amelia Palmer, who became a close friend of Annie during the last years of the latter's life, said that Annie cried telling her about John's death. She had always seemed downcast when talking about her children and how "since the death of her husband she seemed to have given away all together."

* * *

At the time of John's death, Annie was living with a wire-sieve maker named John Sivvey at a common lodging house at 30 Dorset Street. He left her soon afterwards. Common lodging houses (or doss houses as they were referred to by those living in them) were a step down from the furnished rooms like those at 29 Hanbury Street, but they were more bearable for most than the workhouses if only because they offered more freedom. Many of them also allowed men and women to sleep together, making them ideal for the casual "unfortunates" (prostitutes) of the time.

As an experiment in 1886, Hugh Edward Hoare, who would become a member of parliament for Cambridge in the 1890s, took over an East End lodging house. For 18 months he ran the house, seeing for himself the atmosphere that produced so many criminals. He wrote about his findings in the *Cambridge Independent Press*. Although the location of this lodging house was never mentioned, Hoare deliberately chose one of the worst streets, which, at that time, would have been Flower and Dean, Thrawl or Dorset.

"[The street] is dirty, ill-paved and ill-lighted, and it is only just wide enough for one vehicle," Hoare wrote, perhaps describing the very street on which Annie spent her last days. "All the houses, which are dirty and out of repair, are, with the exception of a few which are let out as furnished apartments of the lowest possible kind, registered lodging-houses, and contain from ten to a hundred beds. Over the doors, which generally stand open, and on a canvas screen in front of the lower part of the windows is a notice that a bed may be had for fourpence a night ... I was perfectly conscious myself of a different moral atmosphere when I turned into — Street. I not only saw the difference, but I felt it."

The Common Lodging House Act of 1851 was introduced to bring some semblance of control over the proliferation of these houses. In Whitechapel alone there were 200 common lodging houses, sleeping more than 9000 on any given night. Under the new Act, all houses were to be under police supervision, every room had to be inspected, and the maximum number of lodgers allowed (based on the size of the rooms) had to be displayed at each house. The rooms were to be aired out for two hours each day and a fresh supply of linen given weekly. There were to be separate houses for men and women, with a few rooms set aside for married couples.

However, these rules didn't work and were seldom enforced. In many of the lodging houses, fourpence a night could get you a bed to sleep in. However, for eightpence, a man and woman could get a double bed to do anything but sleep. The owners scoffed at the laws. Common lodging houses were big business and many fortunes were made by their owners. Magistrate Montagu Williams went to see the houses for himself and came away appalled.

"You get a tolerably good clue to the character of these dens even from an external scrutiny," Williams wrote in *Round London: Down East and Up West* in 1884.

"At the windows you see some hideous human heads, male and female, with blotched, bloated and bestial faces, matted and tangled hair, and hungry, desperate eyes."

The following exchange, which appeared in the *East End News* less than a month after Annie's murder, is between Magistrate Williams and a trial witness who was a deputy of a lodging house:

> *Mr. Williams:* How many beds do you make up there?
> *Witness:* Twenty-eight singles and twenty-four doubles.
> *Mr. Williams:* By "doubles" you mean for a man and a woman?
> *Witness:* Yes sir.

Annie Chapman

Williams: And the woman can take any man she likes? You don't know if the couple are married or not?

Witness: No, sir. We don't ask them.

Williams: Precisely what I thought. And the sooner these lodging-houses are put down the better. They are the haunt of the burglar, the home of the pickpocket and the hotbed of prostitution. I don't think I can put it stronger than that. It is time the owners of these places, who reap large profits from them, were looked after.

* * *

Annie Chapman stayed in a number of different common lodging houses throughout 1887 and had been forced to turn to prostitution after her husband died. From May or June 1888 on, she lived consistently at 35 Dorset Street, Spitalfields. This common lodging house was known as Crossingham's and slept approximately 300 people per night.

Dorset Street was infamous in Spitalfields. Running east-west between Commercial and Crispin Streets, it was known locally as "Dossett" Street because of the number of common lodging houses along it. Three public houses (pubs) also lay along its stretch. Directly across the street from Crossingham's was the narrow brick archway entrance to Miller's court which, eight weeks after Annie's murder, would become infamous itself as the scene of the fifth Ripper murder.

Annie was seeing someone regularly in the months before her murder. Known as "the Pensioner", Edward Stanley claimed to be a member of the military. He and Annie often spent weekends together at Crossingham's and he frequently paid for her bed there, as well as that of another resident, Eliza Cooper. Stanley instructed Timothy Donovan, who ran the house, to turn Annie away if she tried to enter with another man.

Sometime in August, while Stanley was away, Annie bumped into her brother, Fontain Smith. She was not on good terms with anyone in her family, but did confide to him that she was hard up, though she would not tell him where she was living. He gave her two shillings for lodgings.

Stanley returned on 1 September, and the following day Annie got in a fight with Eliza Cooper. Annie borrowed a piece of soap from Eliza so that Stanley could get washed, but she didn't return it. An argument over the soap broke out at one of the pubs on the street the next day and continued later back at Crossingham's. Annie was a stout woman, but only about 5 feet tall. And, by all accounts, she was usually very docile. During the argument, Eliza punched Annie in the eye and chest. The next day, Timothy Donovan noticed Annie had a black mark on her head.

"Tim, this is lovely, ain't it," she reportedly told him.

She also met Amelia Palmer near Spitalfields Church

the same day.

"How did you get that?" Palmer asked, pointing to a bruise on her right temple.

In response, Annie opened her dress to show Palmer another bruise on her chest. She said she felt unwell.

When Palmer saw her the next day, her friend looked worse.

"She said she felt no better, and she should go into the casual ward [in a workhouse] for a day or two," Amelia Palmer said. "I remarked that she looked very pale, and asked her if she had had anything to eat. She replied, 'No, I have not had a cup of tea today.' I gave her twopence to get some and told her not to get any rum, of which she was fond."

At this point Annie did, apparently, check herself into a casual ward because Donovan found a bottle of medicine at the lodging house after the murder. It was Friday, 7 September before anyone saw her again. She usually went to Stratford on Fridays to sell her crochet work or flowers – and perhaps to ply her other trade as well.

"I met her about five o'clock in Dorset Street," Palmer said. "She appeared to be perfectly sober. I said 'Are you going to Stratford today?' She answered 'I feel too ill to do anything.'"

Palmer left and returned 10 minutes later to find Annie standing on the same spot.

"She said 'It is of no use giving way. I must pull myself together and go out and get some money or I shall have no lodgings,'" Palmer stated. She didn't know then that she would never see her friend alive again.

At some point that evening, Annie went to see her sister in Vauxhall for money and was given fivepence. She showed up at Crossingham's and asked Donovan for permission to go into the kitchen. He let her. Shortly after midnight she drank a pint of beer with a fellow lodger and then headed out again. On her return at 1.35 a.m., Annie was seen eating a baked potato. John "Brummy" Evans, the elderly night watchman, was sent to her to collect her bed money. She went upstairs to see Donovan in his office.

"I haven't sufficient money for my bed," she told him. "Don't let it. I shan't be long before I am in."

"You can find money for your beer and you can't find money for your bed," he admonished.

She stood in the doorway for a couple of minutes.

"Never mind Tim, I shall soon be back," she said. And turning to Evans, Annie added "I won't be long, Brummy. See that Tim keeps the bed for me."

Evans followed her out and watched her walk down the street.

Annie usually rented the same double bed every night – number 29, Donovan would later tell the inquest. Number 29 would not be lucky for her on this night.

The last sighting of Annie was at 5.30 a.m. Elizabeth Long was walking along Hanbury Street on her way to Spitalfields market.

Annie Chapman

"I passed 29 Hanbury Street," she later testified. "I saw a man and a woman standing on the pavement talking. I saw the woman's face ... I did not see the man's face but I noticed that he was dark. He was wearing a brown low-crowned felt hat. I think he had on a dark coat. By the look of him he seemed to me a man over forty years of age. He appeared to be a little taller than [Annie].

"He looked like a foreigner," she continued. "They were talking pretty loudly. I overheard him say to her 'Will you?' and she replied 'Yes.'"

Long said she often saw couples on the street at that hour and did not pay that much attention to them. She later identified Annie as the woman she saw on the street.

Within half an hour of that sighting, John Davis found Annie Chapman dead.

* * *

It was 6.10 a.m. when Inspector Joseph Chandler, standing at the corner of Hanbury and Commercial Streets, saw men running towards him.

"Another woman has been murdered!" they told him. When he arrived at the scene, the corridor was filled with people, but no one had ventured into the yard. He immediately sent for an ambulance and George Bagster Phillips, divisional surgeon of police. Phillips arrived at 6.30 a.m.

"The left arm was across the left breast, and the legs

were drawn up, the feet resting on the ground, and the knees turned outwards," Phillips said. "The face was swollen and turned on the right side and the tongue protruded between the front teeth, but not beyond the lips; it was much swollen. Small intestines and other portions were lying on the right side of the body on the ground above the right shoulder, but attached. There was a large quantity of blood, with a part of the stomach [lying] above the left shoulder ... The body was cold, except that there was a certain remaining heat, under the intestines, in the body. Stiffness of the limbs was not marked, but it was commencing. The throat was dissevered deeply. I noticed that the incision of the skin was jagged, and reached right round the neck."

Word of the murder had spread quickly and by the time the ambulance arrived, a large crowd was gathering outside in the street. Phillips ordered the body to be taken to the Whitechapel Workhouse Infirmary mortuary where several hundred more people had already gathered.

It was the same mortuary where Polly Nichols had been taken and the same problem occurred – namely, the body was stripped and partly washed before Phillips could arrive to do the post-mortem and search for clues on the clothing. (Wynne Baxter, the coroner for the inquests into both deaths, spoke up immediately when the inquest heard about this: "The fact is that Whitechapel does not possess a mortuary," he said. "The place is not a mortuary at all. We have no right to take a body there. It is simply a shed belonging to the workhouse officials. Juries have over and over again reported the matter to the District Board of Works. The East End, which requires mortuaries more than anywhere else, is most deficient ... [and] a workhouse inmate is not the proper man to take care of a body in such an important matter as this.")

When Inspector Chandler arrived at the mortuary, Annie's body was still on the ambulance. He made note of her clothes and their condition:

- a black figured jacket, which came down to the knees and was hooked at the top and buttoned down the front, with two or three spots of blood on the left sleeve but stained with blood about the neck;
- a long black skirt with very little blood on the outside, at the back, as if she had been lying in it;
- an old and dirty pair of lace-up boots;
- two bodices that were stained very little;
- stockings with no trace of blood on them;
- a white cotton handkerchief with a broad red border tied about her neck; and
- a large pocket, under the skirt and tied about the waist, that was empty and torn down the side and front.

Chandler reported that the rest of the clothes were neither cut nor torn.

Another policeman arrived at the mortuary and wrote down a description of the deceased, who had not yet been identified: "5 feet 0 inches; Stout; Dark wavy brown hair; Blue Eyes; A large thick nose; Fair complexion; Well proportioned; Two teeth missing from the lower jaw."

Donovan and a lodger from Crossingham's both went to the mortuary to view the body. It was lying in the same shell (a roughly made, temporary coffin) that previously held Mary Ann Nichols' remains. They identified the woman as Annie Sivvey, which is how they knew her. Amelia Palmer heard the description of the victim and thought it might be Annie Chapman. *The Star* reported that Palmer "identified her soon after she had been taken to the mortuary as 'Dark Annie', and as she came from the mortuary gate bitterly crying, said between her tears, 'I knowed her; I kissed her poor cold face.'"

Edward Stanley, the Pensioner, heard the rumours of Annie's death and appeared at Crossingham's on the afternoon of 8 September. When he learned it was true, witnesses said he didn't say a word but quickly left.

Phillips arrived at the mortuary to do the post-mortem examination. He made note of the bruises he found from Annie's altercation with Eliza Cooper. There were abrasions over the ring finger, with distinct markings of a ring or rings (Annie had been wearing three copper rings on the last day of her life, but these were missing at the time of her death). The incisions into the skin of the neck had begun on the left side.

There were two distinct clean cuts on the left of the spine.

"The muscular structures appeared as though an attempt had been made to separate the bones of the neck," he testified.

The stomach contained a little food, but no fluid. According to Phillips, there was no appearance of the deceased having drunk alcohol, but there were signs of great deprivation. He was convinced she had not taken any strong alcohol for some hours before her death. He did note Annie was "far advanced in disease of the lungs [tuberculosis] and membranes of the brain", but these may have been symptoms of syphilis and had nothing to do with the cause of death.

Although word of the intestines being pulled out of the body had already circulated, rumours of what else Phillips found heightened the already growing fear among the public. The doctor felt the information should not be made public.

"In giving these details to the public I believe you are thwarting the ends of justice," he stated at the inquest.

The coroner, Wynne Baxter, initially agreed. However, he recalled Phillips a few days later and said the information needed to be on the record, though the press was asked not to print the findings. For the most part, they followed this request. Phillips's autopsy reports disappeared many years ago, but the medical journal *The Lancet* laid bare the details in its 29 September 1888 issue:

"It appears that the abdomen had been entirely laid open; that the intestines, severed from their mesenteric attachments, had been lifted out of the body, and placed on the shoulder of the corpse; whilst from the pelvis, the uterus and its appendages, with the upper portion of the vagina and the posterior two-thirds of the bladder, had been entirely removed. No trace of these parts could be found, and the incisions were cleanly cut, avoiding the rectum, and dividing the vagina low enough to avoid injury to the cervix uteri."

The weapon with which the incisions were inflicted was at least 5 to 6 inches long and must have been very sharp. Phillips said "the mutilation of the body was of such a character as could only have been effected by a practised hand. ... [T]he manner in which they had been done indicated a certain amount of anatomical knowledge." The doctor added that even he would not have been able to do it in less than 15 minutes, and would have been considerably longer if he had done it in a more deliberate and exact way.

Phillips felt that Annie had been dead for about two hours when he first saw her, but acknowledged that he could be wrong in his estimation. It was quite a cool night (7.9°C) and the massive blood loss and exposed abdomen would have cooled the body down very quickly.

The inquest began on 10 September 1888 and took place on five separate days, concluding on 26 September. Most of the testimony presented revolved around the medical evidence and tracing the movements of Annie on her last day alive. Edward Stanley was also located and exposed as a liar and a fraud. He was not a military man at all, but a bricklayer's labourer.

However, he had an alibi for the night of Annie's murder.

In his long summation at the conclusion of the inquest, coroner Baxter talked about the life Annie had lived in the common lodging houses of the area.

"The glimpses of life in these dens which the evidence in this case discloses is sufficient to make us feel that there is much in the nineteenth century civilisation of which we have small reason to be proud," he said.

The medical evidence presented a very clear conclusion.

"There are no meaningless cuts," Baxter stated. "The [uterus] has been taken by one who knew where to find it, what difficulties he would have to contend against, and how he could use his knife so as to abstract the organ without injury to it. No unskilled person could have known where to find it or could have recognised it when it was found."

The jury, not surprisingly, came back with a verdict of "wilful murder against a person or persons unknown".

Annie Chapman was buried on 14 September 1888. Her relatives paid for the funeral and kept it secret. They were the only ones to attend.

In the days and weeks following Annie's murder, fear and revulsion grew in the city. So did the interest. The print run on the evening papers on 8 September was immense. When newsagents ran out, people waited at the shops until the next run showed up. Five policemen were needed to keep those who didn't live there out of 29 Hanbury Street.

"During the whole of Saturday and yesterday a large

crowd congregated in front of the house in Hanbury Street", *The Times* reported, "and the neighbours on either side did much business by making a small charge to persons who were willing to pay it to view from windows the yard in which the murder was committed."

"In the street half a dozen costermongers took up their stand and did a brisk business in fruit and refreshments," the *Manchester Guardian* noted. "Thousands of respectably dressed persons visited the scene and occasionally the road became so crowded that the constables had to clear it by making a series of raids upon the spectators.

"All day nothing else was talked of, even by men who are hardened to seeing a great deal that is brutal," the article continued. "Strong, buxom, muscular women seemed to move in fear and trembling, declaring that they would not dare venture in the streets unaccompanied by their husbands."

"Hideous malice, deadly cunning, insatiable thirst for blood – all these are the marks of the mad homicide," *The Star* proclaimed. "London lies today under the spell of a great terror. A nameless reprobate – half beast, half man – is at large, who is daily gratifying his murderous instincts on the most miserable and defenceless classes of the community."

False reports of arrests were rampant. People picked up on unrelated charges were almost lynched by crowds who believed the police had caught the killer. The police themselves soon wished they had, for criticism of them and their lack of an arrest quickly gained momentum. On 9 September

1888, *The New York Times* opined that "the London police and detective force is probably the stupidest in the world".

"The general feelings of dissatisfaction about the police is [sic] loudly expressed," reported the *Weekly Herald*. "He [the killer] is by no means satisfied yet and it is gruesome to note the settled expectancy with which the people generally speak of 'the next murder'."

The police were simply ill-equipped to deal with a murderer such as this one. Nevertheless, they still believed they could stop him from killing again.

"Last night the police were posted in strong force throughout the neighbourhood," the *Manchester Guardian* reported. "Their precautions are such that they consider it impossible that any further outrage can be perpetrated."

The perpetrator who would shortly become known as Jack the Ripper must have had a good laugh when he read that one.

Did you hear the footsteps behind you
or see the shining knife?
Did you know that the hand at your back
would be the one to take your life?

Chapter 3
Elizabeth Stride

25. Sept. 1888

Dear Boss

I keep on hearing the police have caught me. but they wont fix me just yet. I have laughed when they look so clever and talk about being on the <u>right</u> track. That joke about Leather apron gave me real fits. I am down on whores and I shant quit ripping them till I do get buckled. Grand work the last job was. I gave the lady no time to squeal. How can they catch me now. I love my work and want to start again. You will soon hear of me with my funny little games. I saved some of the proper <u>red</u> stuff in a ginger beer bottle over the last job to write with but it went thick like glue and I cant use it. Red ink is fit enough I hope <u>ha. ha.</u> The next job I do I shall clip the ladys ears off and send to the police officers just for jolly wouldn't you. Keep this letter back till I do a bit more work. then give it out straight My

knife's so nice and sharp I want to get to work right
away if I get a chance
Good luck.
Yours truly
Jack the Ripper

Dont mind me giving the trade name

wasnt good enough to post this before I got all the red
ink off my hands curse it No luck yet. They say I'm a
doctor now <u>ha ha</u>

This "Dear Boss" letter was not addressed to the police department, as one might suspect, but to the editor of the Central News Agency. The newspapers and the police received many hoaxes and fake letters, but this one was a little different because it gave the killer the name of "Jack the Ripper". They did hold it back for a few days, but then it made the news because one of the writer's promises appeared to come true.

"Long Liz" was a teller of tall tales and none was taller than the one she told about the great Thames disaster in 1878. The paddle steamboat *Princess Alice*, named after Queen Victoria's third daughter, was purchased by the London Steamboat Company in 1867 and became one of the most popular passenger steamers on the Thames. One of Londoners' pastimes was to take a day trip up the Thames, stopping at small towns along the way. On 3 September 1878, a warm sunny day, more than 700 people were enjoying the round trip from London Bridge to Sheerness. It was nearing dusk at 8.00 p.m. and the journey was coming to an end. The band was packing up their instruments and the *Princess Alice* was approaching the North Woolwich Pier, but still keeping close to the north shore because of the tide. Shortly before this, a coal ship, the *Bywell Castle*, had left Millwood dock bound for Newcastle. The *Bywell Castle*, moving at half speed down the middle of the river, saw the steamer and steered out of its way. However, the *Princess Alice* suddenly headed across the river towards the pier, assuming the coal boat was moving fast enough to give way. It was a mistake Captain Grinstead of the steamer would not live to regret.

Meanwhile, the collier's captain realised what was about to happen and gave the orders to reverse engines full speed. The order came much too late and the giant steel boat nearly sliced the steamboat in two. Within five minutes, both halves of the paddle steamer had slipped under the waves. A desperate fight for survival began, made much worse by the condition of the River Thames, which at that time was full of untreated sewage and industrial waste. The collier was high out of the water so the steamboat's passengers could not cling to it or climb aboard. A few managed to swim through the filth to shore or cling to floating debris and wait for the rescue boats, but most people didn't. In all, only 69 passengers survived and approximately 640 perished, including

Captain Grinstead, who was found, posthumously, to be at fault for the accident.

Elizabeth (Liz) Stride claimed to be one of those 69 survivors. Years after the disaster, she told everyone that she and her husband had been working on the steamer and that both he and two of her children had been killed. She also used the tragedy to explain something else that obviously bothered her – the missing teeth of her lower left jaw. The teeth were lost and her palate badly damaged, she claimed, while she was scrambling up the steamer's mast to save herself and one of the other passengers accidentally kicked her in the mouth. Liz elicited much sympathy from this sad tale and repeatedly used it to acquire money from the Swedish Church in London. The only problem was that John Stride, Liz's husband, actually died in a workhouse (the couple was no longer together) six years after the disaster. An extensive list of the dead failed to make mention of anyone called "Stride". There was also a fund set up in London at the time of the disaster to provide for the survivors and those who lost family members. Elizabeth Stride's name did not appear on any of the lists of those who applied for money from this fund, which she most certainly would have done if she were eligible.

Liz also claimed to be from Sweden, and that part of her story was true. Born in Torslanda on 17 November 1843, she moved to Gothenburg when she was 18 years old and began working as a domestic servant. In March 1865, the Gothenburg Police registered her as a prostitute, and a month later Liz gave birth to a still-born girl. Later that year she was hospitalised twice for venereal disease and the law required her to report to the police every few days. In hospital entries on 14 November 1865, she was declared healthy, and in February 1866 she applied to move to the Swedish parish in London. There she entered the London register as an unmarried woman at the Swedish Church in Prince's Square, St. Georges in the East, on 10 July 1866.

Depending on who she was talking to, Liz either came to London in the service of a "foreign gentleman", or she had family in London and "came to see the country". She married John Thomas Stride, 22 years her senior, on 7 March 1869. The couple lived on East India Dock Road, Poplar, and John had a coffee shop on Chrisp Street. In 1871, they moved the shop and themselves to 178 Poplar High Street and stayed there until the shop was taken over by John Dale in 1874. At the end of 1881, with her marriage over, Liz was admitted to the Whitechapel Workhouse Infirmary with bronchitis and then to the workhouse itself on her recovery. John Stride died of heart failure at the Poplar Sick Asylum in 1884.

By 1885 Liz had moved in with Michael Kidney, with whom she had a stormy, sometimes violent, relationship. Liz charged Kidney with assault in April 1887, but then failed to appear at Thames Magistrates Court. The charges were dropped. Her pattern was to leave him for a few days or weeks and then return. "It was drink that made her go away," Kidney would later state. "She always returned without me going after her. I think she liked me better than any other man."

When she left Kidney, Liz would stay at a lodging house at 32 Flower and Dean Street. A worker at the house said of her that a "better hearted, more good natured cleaner woman never lived." This sentiment was echoed by the night watchman: "Lor' bless you, when she could get no work she had to do the best she could for her living, but a neater, cleaner woman never lived." Other residents said she was a "very quiet" and "sober" woman – perhaps a stretching of the truth not unlike what Liz herself was capable of.

During 1887 and 1888, Liz Stride was convicted eight times for drunkenness. Kidney was not immune to the law either, having been sent down for three days in July 1888 on charges of being drunk and disorderly and using obscene language.

In September 1888, Liz received money twice from the Swedish Church. On the 25th of that month, Kidney saw her for the last time. He assumed she would be home when he returned from work, but she had left him, yet again, and moved back to 32 Flower and Dean Street. The people there hadn't seen her for three months and she told a fellow resident that she had "had words with the man she was living with."

The following evening, the lodging house was visited by Dr Thomas Barnardo, who walked into the kitchen to talk with some of the residents. Barnardo, born in Ireland in 1845, had come to London years earlier to train as a doctor. Appalled at the conditions in which East End children were living, he set up a school for them in 1867, and then, in 1870, opened his first home for boys. He often visited lodging houses to gather information and on 26 September 1888, his focus was on the murders.

"I had been examining many of the common lodging houses in Bethnal-green that night," Barnardo wrote in a letter to *The Times*, dated 6 October 1888. "The company soon recognised me, and the conversation turned upon the previous murders. The female inmates of the kitchen seemed thoroughly frightened at the dangers to which they were presumably exposed." Barnardo told them of his ideas "by which children at all events could be saved from the con- tamination of the common lodging houses and the streets ... [M]y remarks were manifestly followed with deep interest by all the women."

Talk returned to the recent murders. "One poor crea- ture, who had evidently been drinking", he wrote, "exclaimed somewhat bitterly to the following effect: 'we're all up to no good, and no one cares what becomes of us. Perhaps some of us will be killed next!' And then she added, 'If anybody had helped the likes of us long ago we would never have come to this!'" Barnardo, who would briefly be considered as a suspect in the murders himself because he was a doctor, later identified Liz Stride as one of the women sitting in the kitchen that evening.

Liz was still living at the lodging house three days after Barnardo's visit. It was Saturday, 29 September 1888, and in the afternoon she cleaned some of the rooms and was paid sixpence by Elizabeth Tanner, the house's deputy. The two had a drink at the Queen's Head public house and then walked home together. When Liz left the house again before 8.00 p.m., she still had her sixpence with her.

Saturday evening in Whitechapel was always the busiest night of the week. It was payday. This was the night when "the unfortunates" would be most active, knowing that men had a little extra money in their pockets. Many of these women prostituted themselves for glasses of gin (threepence a glass), so many of them would also be heavily under the influence of alcohol and would more easily succumb to the killer. "An Autumn Evening in Whitechapel", in *Littell's Living Age* for 3 November 1888, paints a grim picture of an average evening in the area where Jack's victims had lived:

> *Since these outrages [murders] the dark places of Whitechapel and Spitalfields have undoubtedly been a little darker and stiller, and more depressing. Some streets have presented, even to those familiar with them, quite a desolate and deserted appearance after nightfall ... Turn down this side street out of the main Whitechapel Road ... [and it] is oppressively dark, though at present the gloom is relieved somewhat by feebly lighted shop fronts. Men are lounging at the doors of the shops, smoking evil-smelling pipes ... It is getting on into the night, but*

gutters, and doorways, and passages, and staircases appear to be teeming with children.

In describing Buck's Row (the scene of Polly Nichols' murder), the article went on to say it "looks to be a singularly desolate, out-of-the-way region. But there is a piano-organ grinding out the 'Men of Harlech' over the spot where the murdered woman was found; women and girls are freely coming and going through the darkness, and the rattle of sewing-machines, and the rushing of railway trains, and the noisy horseplay of a gang of boys, all seem to be combining with the organ-grinder to drown recollection and to banish all unpleasant reflection."

That Saturday was windy and wet as Liz Stride headed out again. The watchman at the lodging house said she looked quite cheerful as she passed him by the door, somewhere between 7.00 and 8.00 p.m. Two labourers entering a nearby pub at about 11.00 p.m. later testified they saw Liz leaving with a man who, at 5 feet, 5 inches tall, was the same height as she was. He wore a morning suit and a billycock (bowler) hat. "It was raining very fast", one of the labourers said, "and they did not appear willing to go out. He was hugging and kissing her, and as he seemed a respectably dressed man, we were rather astonished at the way he was going on at the woman."

By 11.45 p.m. it had stopped raining. William Marshall, outside his house at 64 Berner Street, saw Liz standing with a man a few doors away. This man was 5 feet, 6 inches tall, stout, middle-aged and wore dark pants, a peaked sailor-like cap and a short black cutaway coat. They were talking and kissing and as they walked past Marshall, the man said, with an English accent, "You would say anything but your prayers", to which Liz had laughed in reply. Police Constable Smith would be the next to see Liz in the early hours of Sunday when he spotted her with a young man on Berner Street, opposite the International Workingmen's Educational Club (IWEC). The IWEC, at 40 Berner Street, was an old wooden house converted for use as a social club and capable of holding over 200 people. As described in the *Illustrated Police News* of 6 October 1888, it was "an offshoot of the Socialist League, and a rendezvous of a number of foreign residents, chiefly Russians, Poles and continental Jews of various nationalities". Adjacent to the left side of the club was a passageway leading from Berner Street (later renamed Henriques Street) to Dutfield's Yard.

According to Constable Smith, the man he saw with Liz was about 28 years old and stood about 5 feet, 7 inches tall. He was wearing dark pants, an overcoat and a hard felt deer-stalker hat. Only 5 or 10 minutes after Smith's sighting, Israel Schwartz, as he later recalled, turned into Berner Street and saw a man stop and speak to Liz. They were close to the passageway leading to Dutfield's Yard. The man, said Schwartz, tried to pull Liz into the street, and in doing so turned her around and threw her to the ground. She screamed, but not loudly. Schwartz also noticed a second man on the opposite side of the road, lighting his pipe. When the man who had assaulted Liz saw Schwartz, he shouted "Lipski!" at him and Schwartz hurried away. (In 1887, a Jewish man named Israel Lipski had been found guilty of forcibly poisoning a young girl and was hanged. The case set off a wave of anti-Semitism and the name "Lipski" became a verbal slur throughout the East End.) The man who threw Liz down, said Schwartz, was about 5 feet, 5 inches tall and 30 years old, with broad shoulders. He also had a small brown moustache and was wearing dark pants, a black cap with a peak, and a dark jacket. The man lighting the pipe, Schwartz estimated, was 5 feet, 11 inches tall and 35 years old, with light brown hair and wearing a dark overcoat with an old black hard, felt hat with a wide brim.

Sifting through numerous eyewitness descriptions did not make the police's task easy at any time during the investigation, but these details became especially important because, as many Ripperologists today believe, one of these two men was very likely the killer.

Although the police believed Schwartz and the descriptions he gave, he was never called as a witness at the inquest. It could have been that the authorities didn't want the description of the suspect broadcast, which might thwart efforts to catch him. Whatever the reason Schwartz wasn't called was never made clear.

Friendly discussions of mutual interest were customary at the IWEC on Saturday nights. On this Saturday night, the talk was around the necessity for socialism amongst Jews. At 11.00 p.m. the discussion broke up and a large part of the crowd left. Those remaining began to entertain themselves with songs. The leader of the debate that evening, Morris Eagle, left to take his girlfriend home but came back at 12.40 a.m. Finding the front door of the club locked, he walked down the passageway to another entrance off Dutfield's Yard. From there he could hear a friend singing upstairs at the club, but – as he later testified – he saw and heard nothing else. Lewis Diemschutz, however, did. Diemschutz was the club's steward and lived on the IWEC premises with his wife. He was also a hawker of cheap jewellery and every Saturday took his wares to market in a two-wheeled barrow pulled by a pony. At 1.00 a.m., ending a long day at the market, Diemschutz had just turned his pony into the passageway leading to Dutfield's Yard.

"For a distance of eighteen or twenty feet from the street, there is a dead wall on each side of the court [passageway], the effect of which is to shroud the intervening space in absolute darkness after sunset," the *Illustrated Police News* reported. "Further back some light is thrown into the court from the windows of a workmen's club, which occupies the whole length of the court on the right, and from a number of cottages, occupied mainly by tailors and cigarette makers on the left."

By the time Diemschutz pulled into the passageway, however, the lights in all of the dwelling houses were out.

"All at once my pony shied at some object on the right," Diemschutz told the inquest. When the pony would not go forward, "I looked to see what the object was, and observed that there was something unusual, but could not tell what. It was a dark object. I put my whip handle to it, and tried to lift it up, but as I did not succeed I jumped down from my barrow and struck a match." It was very windy, but in the brief light from the flame before it was extinguished, he saw a figure lying there. "I could tell from the dress it was a woman." He left the jittery pony outside and raced into the club to check on his wife. "All I did was to run indoors and ask where my missus was because she is of a weak constitution, and I did not want to frighten her."

Seeing his wife was safe, Diemschutz then ran to the front room of the club where he told the several members still there that a woman was lying in the yard – "though I could not say whether she was drunk or dead. I then got a candle and went into the yard, where I could see blood before I reached the body."

Another slit throat, another dead woman. This time, though, the body was still warm and the blood still running. Jack, it seems, had been interrupted in his work. Diemschutz himself said later he believed the killer had still been in the yard when he pulled in, given the continuing odd behaviour of his pony. When questioned, none of the nearby residents reported hearing anything but the singing coming from the club. That very music and the proximity of the club members likely gave the victim a false sense of security.

Within minutes, the police were summoned and spectators descended on the scene. Constable Henry Lamb entered the club and "examined the hands and clothes of all the members". He found no blood on them and, on looking through the premises, found no blood present there either. Dr Frederick William Blackwell arrived to examine the body at 1.16 a.m. and said later that the victim had been dead for only 20 to 30 minutes before he arrived.

"The neck and chest were quite warm, as were also the legs, and the face was slightly warm," Blackwell swore at the inquest. "The hands were cold. The right hand was open and on the chest, and was smeared with blood. The left hand lying on the ground, was partially closed, and contained a small packet of cachous [small lozenges used by smokers to sweeten their breath] wrapped in tissue paper ... [T]he incision in the neck commenced on severing the vessels on that side, cutting the windpipe completely in two, and terminating on the opposite side 1 1/2 inches below the angle of the right jaw, but without severing the vessels on that side."

Detective-Inspector Edmund Reid sent two of his inspectors to the site at 1.25 a.m. and Dr George Phillips, who handled the two previous victims, arrived shortly after 1.30 a.m. Reid himself and Superintendent Thomas Arnold, head of H division (Whitechapel) of the Metropolitan Police, followed shortly. The police, having learned from their past mistakes, had the victim taken to St. George's in the East mortuary, where two doctors oversaw the post-mortem autopsy. No one recognised the woman who had been wearing a long black cloth jacket, fur trimmed around the bottom, with a red rose and white maiden hair fern pinned to it. (Liz, witnesses later said, had not been wearing flowers when she left the lodging house.) A black crepe bonnet had been found lying near the body. The post-mortem results echoed those for the previous two victims, with the doctors stating that they were sure this victim's throat had not been cut while she was standing up. As a result of discussions at the inquest surrounding the *Princess Alice* disaster and Liz Stride's involvement in it (or not), the doctors re-examined the body and reported they found no damage whatsoever to the victim's soft or hard palate – contrary to what Liz had told everyone.

The question of her name and identification also became a story worthy of Liz herself. Many people viewed the body and recognised a woman they knew only as "Long Liz". The name "Elizabeth Stride" surfaced but could not be confirmed. Then along came a Mrs Mary Malcom who muddied the waters completely. She asked to see the body on Sunday, 30 September, but could not identify it. Twice she returned and finally claimed the woman was her sister, Mrs Elizabeth Watts. On the same day, Michael Kidney identified the body as Elizabeth Stride, as did Constable Walter Stride, nephew to John who had been married to the victim. Nevertheless, Mary Malcolm's identification took precedence because she claimed to be the closest blood relative and

Kidney was not married to Stride. She testified on the second day of the inquest, 2 October, and painted a very unsavoury picture of her sister, all the while sobbing and looking pained. She claimed that for three years she had seen this person, her sister, every Saturday and gave her two shillings for lodging. Among other things, she said Elizabeth Watts was often "worse for drink" and had often been charged with drunkenness; that her husband left her after he caught her with a porter; and that Watts once left a naked, illegitimate baby at Malcolm's doorstep to be looked after until she returned to get it. When asked by the coroner what her sister did for a livelihood, Malcom replied grimly, "I had my doubts." Malcom also swore that her sister's spirit had come to her the night of the murder and kissed her on the cheek. This, she said, told her that Watts was dead.

Then, on the last day of the inquest, 23 October, the real Mrs Elizabeth Stokes (Watts) showed up to testify. She was not happy, declaring, "I want to clear my character. My sister I have not seen for years. She has given me a dreadful character. Her evidence is all false ... This has put me to a dreadful trouble and trial. I have only a poor crippled husband, who is now outside. It is a shame my sister should say what she has said about me, and that the innocent should suffer for the guilty." By the time she gave her testimony, however, it had clearly been established that the victim was Elizabeth Stride. Coroner Wynne Baxter felt the inquest had been unnecessarily delayed by "the need to investigate her [Stride's] own

extraordinary lies about her past and Mrs Malcolm's errone-
ous identification of her with Mrs Elizabeth Stokes".

Michael Kidney did not take the murder well at all. On 1
October, he entered the Leman Street Police Station and, very
drunk, said that if he had been the policeman on whose beat
Elizabeth had been murdered, he would have shot himself.
He then asked to see a detective. He was not in much better
shape when he testified at the inquest two days later. In a
long, rambling interchange with the coroner, Kidney insisted
he had vital information and if he had been allowed to have
a detective at his disposal for a day he would have solved the
murders already. Asked what information he had, he reiter-
ated his demand for a detective. When that was declined, he
said he would keep the information to himself.

Elizabeth Stride was buried at the East London Cemetery on 6 October 1888. The small funeral was paid for by
the parish.

In one way, Liz Stride was lucky that Jack had been
interrupted in his work because it meant her body was still
intact. Catherine Eddowes would not be as fortunate. "The
murderer in ELIZABETH STRIDE'S case had no more than
time to inflict the fatal wound," *The Times* reported on 1
October 1888. "He was then interrupted, but he was not so to
be put off from the completion of his abominable design."

Chapter 4
Catherine Eddowes

Catherine (Kate) Eddowes was attracting quite a crowd at 8.00 p.m. on Saturday, 29 September 1888. Holding court in Aldgate High Street, a drunken Kate had been entertaining onlookers with imitations of a fire engine. Then she lay down on the pavement and went to sleep.

City of London Constable Lewis Robinson noticed the group of people "surrounding a woman" who was drunk and lying on the "footway", he later stated. "I asked the crowd if any of them knew her or where she lived, but got no answer," Robinson said. "I then picked her up and sat her against the shutters, but she fell down sideways. With the aid of a fellow constable I took her to Bishopsgate Police Station. There she was asked her name, and she replied 'Nothing'. She was then put into a cell." It wasn't surprising no one recognised Kate, because she had walked out of Whitechapel, which was under the supervision of Scotland Yard, and into the City of London. It was not an area she frequented often. Constable George Hutt came on duty at 9.45 p.m. that night and checked on the prisoners every half hour after that, reporting that at 12.15 a.m., he heard Kate singing softly to herself in her cell.

"I visited her several times until five minutes to one on Sunday morning," Hutt said. "I was directed ... to see if any of the prisoners were fit to be discharged. I found [Kate] sober, and after she had given her name and address, she was allowed to leave."

"What time is it?" she asked Hutt, before going.

"Too late for you to get anything to drink," he replied, adding that it was 1.00 a.m.

"I shall get a damn fine hiding when I get home," she told him.

"And serve you right," he replied. "You have no right to get drunk." As he watched Kate walk down the corridor and open the door to leave the station, Hutt asked her to close it after her.

"All right," Kate replied. "Good night, old cock." Hutt watched her pull the door to within a foot of being closed and then she turned to the left. This was not in the direction of the lodging house on Flower and Dean Street where she said she lived, but heading back to Aldgate High Street, where she had been arrested. On the way, Kate would have passed the entrance to Duke Street, at the end of which was Church Passage, leading to Mitre Square. It was a small, enclosed square on the edge of the City. Access to the square was obtained by either a broad, lighted opening from Mitre Street or two footpaths, one of which was Church Passage. The square was poorly lit and usually deserted after dark. On site were a few warehouses, some with a resident caretaker, and a number of private residences. Most of them were derelict. The only occupied private residence in the square was home to a policeman and his family.

It was 1.44 a.m. when Constable Edward Watkins approached Mitre Square via Mitre Street. He only had a small area to cover on his beat and all had been quiet when he last checked the square at 1.30 a.m. His lantern was on and fixed to his belt so he immediately saw the body to his right, lying in the square. "The woman was on her back, with her feet towards the square," Watkins recalled at the inquest. "Her clothes were thrown up. I saw her throat was cut and the stomach ripped open. She was lying in a pool of blood."

Speaking to the press, however, the 17-year veteran of the force was much more graphic. "She was ripped up like a pig in the market," Watkins told a newspaper. "The murderer had inserted the knife just under the nose, cut the nose completely from the face, at the same time inflicting a dreadful gash down the right cheek to the angle of the jawbone. The nose was laid over on the cheek. A more dreadful sight I never saw; it quite knocked me over."

Watkins ran to the door of Kearley and Tonge's tea ware-house in Mitre Square and pounded on it. The night watch-man, George Morris, was sweeping the floor in the direction of the door at the time. "The constable said, 'For God's sake, mate, come to my assistance!'" Morris told the inquest. "I said, 'Stop till I get my lamp. What is the matter?'"

"Oh, dear!" Watkins had replied, "Here is another woman cut to pieces!"

Interrupted in his work on Liz Stride, the killer this time took his rage out on Catherine Eddowes.

Born in Wolverhampton in 1842, Catherine (Kate) Eddowes was the most educated of Jack's five confirmed vic-tims and the one with the most stable home life at the time of her murder. Relatives described her when she was younger as a "very good looking and jolly sort of girl." Kate left school at 13 when her mother died, but she eventually returned to finish her education while caring for an aunt. By the age of 21, Kate had become involved with Thomas Conway, an older man who drew a pension from the 18th Royal Irish Foot Regiment. Although there was no definitive proof, Kate claimed they had been married. They had three children together and she had his initials tattooed on her forearm. They earned a living selling chapbooks (small pamphlets of ballads and tales) that Conway penned. The couple also wrote and sold gallows bal-lads. Kate reportedly hawked one such ballad at the execution of her own cousin, Christopher Robinson, hanged in January 1866 for murdering his fiancée by cutting her throat!

Catherine Eddowes

They separated in 1880, with Kate taking custody of her daughter, Annie, and Conway taking the two sons. Annie later said the break-up was the result of her mother's drinking, but Kate's sister, Elizabeth, said it was because of Conway's drinking and abuse. In 1881, Kate met John Kelly at Cooney's common lodging house at 55 Flower and Dean Street. The deputy at the lodging house, Frederick Wilkinson, told the inquest the couple "lived on very good terms. They sometimes had a few words when Kate was in drink, but they were not serious. I believe she got her living by hawking about the streets and cleaning amongst the Jews in Whitechapel. Kelly paid me pretty regularly. Kate was not often in drink. She was a very jolly woman, always singing. Kelly was not in the habit of drinking, and I never saw him worse for drink."

Kelly talked about his relationship with Kate to *The Star* newspaper a couple of days after her murder in 1888. "It is nigh on to seven years since I met Kate, and it was in this very lodging house I first set eyes on her," he was quoted as saying. "We got throwed together a good bit, and the result was that we made a regular bargain ... Kate and me lived on here as best we could. She got a job charing now an [sic] then, and I picked up all the odd jobs I could in Spitalfields Market."

He broke down with emotion a few times during the interview, saying, "I have lived with that girl a long while, and we never quarrelled."

Kate's daughter, Annie, had married a lampblack (pigment made from soot) packer named Louis Phillips and, in

1887, Kate nursed her daughter through a "confinement" (pregnancy). Because of Kate's drinking and appeals for money, that would be the last visit between mother and daughter. Annie moved and did not give her mother their new address.

As many impoverished couples did each year, Kate and John travelled to Kent in September 1888 to work picking the hops used in making malt liquor. On this trip they did not make much money and headed back to Whitechapel. "We didn't get on any too well and started to hoof it home," Kelly told *The Star*. "We came along in company with another man and woman who had worked in the same fields, but who parted with us ... [T]he woman said to Kate, 'I have got a pawn ticket for a flannel shirt. I wish you'd take it, since you're going up to town [London] and it may fit your old man'. So, Kate took it and [it was] in the name of Emily Burrell. We did not have money enough to keep us going till we got to town, but we did get there and came straight to this house [55 Flower and Dean]. Luck was dead set against us."

They reached London on 27 September and slept at the Show Lane Casual Ward that night. The next day Kelly managed to earn sixpence. Kate insisted he take fourpence of it and get a single bed at Cooney's. She took the other twopence and went to the Mile End Casual Ward. She returned at 8.00 a.m. Saturday morning, telling Kelly there was some trouble at the casual ward and she had been turned out early.

"I had nothing but a pair of boots that would bring

anything [to pawn], and I says to her, 'We'll pop the boots and have a bite to eat anyway'," Kelly told *The Star* of that last morning together. He said he persuaded Kate to take his boots to a pawn shop and she received two shillings and six-pence for them and gave her name as Jane Kelly.

Pawn shops were the means of last resort to the poor who did not want to resort to prostitution. Charles Dickens toured the East End extensively and his visits to the abundant pawn shops were the foundation for his seedy depiction of one in *A Christmas Carol*. On payday, the pawn shops filled up as the poor redeemed the items they had pawned earlier in the week (often their best clothes, which they needed for church on Sunday morning). Then on Monday they would return the items to the pawn shop for money and the cycle would start again.

Kate tucked the pawn ticket away with the one given to her by Emily Burrell and returned to Cooney's. These two tickets would be instrumental in identifying her later. With the money from the boots, Kate and Kelly bought tea, cof-fee, sugar and food. They ate their last meal together at the lodging house between 10.00 and 11.00 a.m. that Saturday, 29 September. By the afternoon, Kate and Kelly were again broke and Kate said she would go and find her daughter in Bermondsey to try and get money from her for their lodgings that night. It was 2.00 p.m. and she promised Kelly she would be back by 4.00 p.m.

"I begged her to be back early, for we had been talking

about the Whitechapel murders, and I said I did not want to have that knife get at her," Kelly told *The Star*. "Don't you fear for me," she told Kelly. "I'll take care of myself, and I shan't fall into his hands."

When she did not show up at the lodging house later that night, Kelly was not concerned. He had been told by a local resident that the police had picked Kate up because "she had had a drop to drink" and he believed she would be released Sunday morning. He had no way of knowing she had been freed at 1.00 a.m.

Three men who left the Imperial Club on Duke Street at 1.30 a.m. were later to report that about four minutes later they saw a man and a woman talking together at the corner of Duke Street and Church Passage. Only one of the three took a close look. "The woman was standing with her face towards the man, and I only saw her back," Joseph Lawende stated at the inquest. "She had one hand on his breast. He was the taller. She had on a black jacket and bonnet. I have seen the articles at the police station and believe them to be those the deceased was wearing." It was dark and Lawende admitted he would not be able to point out the man to police. However, given that the victim was found 10 minutes later, Lawende's description of the person he saw was one of the best to date of the killer. He was, Lawende guessed, about 30 years old and 5 feet, 7 inches tall, with a medium build. He had a fair complexion and a moustache, and on that night was wearing a salt-and-pepper-coloured jacket, a grey cloth cap with a peak of the same colour, and a reddish handker-chief knotted around his neck.

Among the most enduring aspects of the Jack the Ripper mystery are the speed and efficiency of his acts of violence and the sheer boldness he displayed in his crimes. What he managed to do to Kate Eddowes in the less than 10 minutes before she was discovered at 1.44 a.m. would only add to his legend. The victim was pronounced dead at 2.00 a.m. by Dr George Sequeira, who waited for the arrival of Dr Gordon Brown, City of London Police Surgeon. Brown found her lying on her back, "arms by the side of the body, as if they had fallen there", Brown wrote in his report. "Both palms were upwards, the fingers slightly bent. A thimble was lying near. The clothes were thrown up ... [and the] abdomen exposed. The intestines were drawn out to a large extent and placed over the right shoulder – they were smeared over with some feculent matter. A piece of about two feet was quite detached from the body and placed between the body and left arm, apparently by design ... [T]he crime must have been committed within half an hour, or certainly within forty minutes from the time when I saw the body," Brown told the inquest. "The face was very much mutilated, the eyelids, the nose, the jaw, the cheeks, the lips, and the mouth all bore cuts ... [and] the throat was cut across to the extent of six or seven inches."

As with all the other victims, "there were no traces of recent connexion [intercourse]". However, the killer would go one step further than he had with Annie Chapman: most of the uterus plus the left kidney were cut out and nowhere to be found. "The peritoneal lining was cut through on the left side and the left kidney carefully taken out and removed," Brown stated. "The left renal artery was cut through. I would say that someone who knew the position of the kidney must have done it." Brown said the killer used a sharp knife, at least 6 inches long, and must have had considerable knowledge as to the position of the abdominal organs. In addition to doctors, he agreed, someone used to cutting up animals would have the expertise to do such a thing.

Most of the victims wore many layers of clothes because they carried with them everything they owned. In pockets attached to their inner clothing, they carried their valuables, such as they were. Kate was no exception. Among the items found on her body were: two short black clay pipes; a tin box containing tea, another one containing sugar and an empty tin matchbox; a piece of red flannel with pins and needles in it; six pieces of soap; a small-toothed comb; a white-handled table knife; a metal spoon; a red leather cigarette case with white metal fillings; buttons and a thimble; a printed handbill; a portion of a pair of spectacles; and a mustard tin containing two pawn tickets, one in the name of Emily Burrell for a man's flannel shirt and the other in the name of Jane Kelly for a pair of men's boots.

The body was taken to the Golden Lane mortuary. When it was stripped, a piece of ear dropped from the clothing.

Inspector Collard itemised Kate's clothes and other posses-sions and also noticed that a large section of the apron the victim had been wearing was missing, severed by a large cut.

Before this second murder of the night (so close on the heels of Liz Stride's murder), the focus had been on the City of London. At 2.55 a.m. it would shift back to Whitechapel and the hands of the Metropolitan Police. That was when Constable Alfred Long, on duty in Goulston Street, Whitechapel, found a portion of a white apron. "There were recent stains of blood on it," he told the inquest. The apron was lying in the passage leading to the staircase of Nos. 106 to 119, a model dwelling house. Above on the wall was writ-ten in chalk, 'The Jews are the men that will not be blamed for nothing'."

Although there has been much confusion through the years over the order of the words, Metropolitan Police Commissioner Charles Warren also wrote down the words and his version agreed with Long's. Long did admit that he might have spelled the word "Jews" differently than it was on the wall. (Warren's version had the word spelled "Jewes" and other ver-sions that have survived through the years include "Juwes".)

After Constable Long searched the staircases and sur-rounding area, he left another constable to stand guard while he took the bloodied piece of apron to the Commercial Street police station. It was soon found to match up with the cut in the apron worn by the Mitre Square murder victim. The assumption was made that the killer had used the apron to wipe his hands after the killing and then discarded it, but Long had passed the same area at 2.20 a.m. and the apron had not been there at that time. Goulston Street was also not close by, so the killer would have had to carry the apron some distance before throwing it away. There seemed to be a missing hour and a half between when the second murder was committed and when the bloodied apron showed. What did the killer do in the meantime?

The other question was who wrote the graffiti on the wall? As the area was largely populated by Jews, it was highly unlikely they would have done it. With police swarming the area in search of the killer that night, Thomas Arnold, Superintendent of Police Division H in Whitechapel, felt he had to act quickly. He sent an Inspector to Goulston Street with a sponge and orders to stand by to rub out the message. There had been an anti-Semitic outburst after Annie Chapman's murder when a Jew was briefly considered as the main suspect and Arnold did not want a repeat. The East End was in a panic over the murders and looking for a scapegoat and Arnold was afraid they would find one in the Jews, causing a riot. He had the support of Metropolitan Police Commissioner Warren when the two met on that Sunday morning, 30 September, shortly before 5.00 a.m.

"I considered it desirable that I should decide the matter myself, as it was one involving so great a responsibility whether any action was taken or not," Warren wrote to the Home Secretary a few weeks later. "... I do not hesitate myself to say that if that writing had been left there would have been an onslaught upon the Jews, property would have been wrecked, and lives would probably have been lost; and I was much gratified with the promptitude with which Superintendent Arnold was prepared to act in the matter if I had not been there."

Warren was there, however, and discussed the various options with those present. Most of the stairs near the wall with the graffiti led to tenements occupied by Jews and the police felt the writing was meant to shed suspicion on them and away from the real killer. With daylight fast approaching, the police would be able to photograph the wall, but it also meant the streets would be teeming with people and, like Arnold, Warren feared a riot. He quickly wiped the message from the wall – an action that would later bring a wrath of criticism down on him by a public already holding him responsible for not catching the killer.

Even without the chalked message, however, suspicion still fell on Jewish residents. The following appeared in the *Jewish Chronicle* on 12 October 1888: "We are authorised by Dr Gordon Brown to state, with reference to a suggestion that the City and Whitechapel murders were the work of a Jewish slaughterer, that he had examined the knives used by the Jewish slaughterers, and he is thoroughly satisfied that none of them could have been used."

The Mitre Square victim still had to be identified. She appeared to be about 40 years of age and 5 feet tall, with dark auburn hair and hazel eyes. She also had "TC" tattooed on her arm.

As dawn broke, John Kelly believed Kate was still safely locked up. "So on Sunday morning I wandered round in the crowds that had been gathered by the talk about the two fresh murders," Kelly told *The Star*. "I stood and looked at the very spot where my poor old gal had laid with her body all cut to pieces and I never knew it."

By Tuesday morning, 2 October, Kelly was becoming worried about Kate's absence. After another long day at the market, he sat down and picked up *The Star* newspaper. "I read down a bit and my eye caught the name of Burrell," he said. "Then it came over me all at once. The tin box, the two pawn tickets, the one for the flannel shirt and the other for my boots. But could Kate have lost them? I read a little further. 'The woman had the letter[s] TC, in Indian ink, on her arm'. Man, you could have knocked me down with a feather. It was my Kate, and no other."

Kelly went to the police station. Neither he nor Kate's sister, Eliza, could understand what she had been doing in Mitre Square. They both swore she would never solicit. The deputy at their lodging house said Kate was always home by 8.00 or 9.00 p.m. and no one there had ever seen her with any man other than Kelly. However, it seems she must have been an occasional "unfortunate", for she had no money when she left Kelly that day to go to her daughter's (who, unknown to Kate, had moved to escape her mother's requests for money) and yet she was found drunk a few hours later by police.

* * *

What became known as the "Saucy Jacky" postcard was received at the Central News Agency on 1 October 1888. It read:

> *I was not codding dear old Boss when I gave you the tip, you'll hear about Saucy Jacky's work tomorrow double event this time number one squealed a bit couldn't finish straight off. ha not the time to get ears for police. thanks for keeping last letter back till I got to work again.*
> *Jack the Ripper*

The handwriting in it was similar to that in the "Dear Boss" letter. It also made reference to the earlier letter (which had not yet been published), to the double murder of the previous evening, and to the victim's ears. This was proof enough for some investigators to be convinced of the postcard's authenticity, given that the "Dear Boss" letter and the details of the double murder did not reach the newspapers until just that morning. However, many still felt both communiqués were a hoax, noting that because the post in London in those days was delivered the same day it was mailed, the sender could have gleaned the information from early editions of the newspapers and then written the letters – not written the letters *before* significant details were published.

Whether or not the letter and postcard were from the real killer, they forever branded him with the self-ascribed moniker of Jack the Ripper. The police hoped that by publishing the correspondence someone would recognise the handwriting and turn in the killer. Instead it made their job more difficult when both they and the press became deluged with fake letters, all of which had to be followed up.

There was one other communication, however, that the police did take seriously, even though the writer did not sign it Jack the Ripper.

As a result of the murders, several community organisations had sprung up. The most prominent was the Mile End Vigilance Committee, formed on 10 September 1888, with George Lusk as its president. On Monday, 15 October, a man walked in to a shop on Mile End Road and asked the shop girl for George Lusk's address. She gave him the street name, but not the house number. The next evening at 8.00 p.m., Lusk received by post a 3-inch-square cardboard box wrapped in brown paper. It was addressed without the house number. Inside the box was a rancid piece of flesh and the following letter:

> *From Hell*
> *Mr Lusk*
> *Sor*
> *I send you half the kinde I took from one woman*

prasarved it for you tother piece I fried and ate and
it was very nise I may send you the bloody knif that
took it out if you only wate a whil longer
signed   Catch me when you can
Mishter Lusk

During the month since the formation of the vigilance committee, Lusk had received many letter hoaxes and assumed this was just another one. Still, he was unsettled enough by it that he told committee members about the package at their meeting the next night, 17 October. The following morning, at the urging of several members, Lusk took the box to a doctor who identified the object as being part of a human kidney. After this was confirmed by a couple more doctors, the group decided to go to the police.

In the end, the Criminal Investigation Department, headed by Robert Anderson, concluded that the package and the two main letters of interest were pranks. Anderson later even added that he thought the letter and Saucy Jack postcard were the work of an enterprising journalist.

* * *

In the days following Kate's murder, the panic in the East End reached feverish levels. This affected the trade for most businesses, including that of the "unfortunates", although many of them were still out on the streets. "A woman who was out in the small hours of the morning was asked, 'Aren't you afraid to be out at this time?'" *The Star* reported on 3 October 1888. "She replied, 'No; the murders are shocking, but we have no place to go, so we're compelled to be out looking for our lodgings.' Another woman in reply to a similar question said 'Afraid? No. I'm armed. Look here,' and she drew a knife from her pocket. She further declared, 'I'm not the only one armed. There's plenty more carry knives now.'" A sadder response came from one unfortunate when she was asked if she was afraid the killer would get her. "I hope he does get me," she replied. "I'm sick of this life."

Catherine (Kate) Eddowes was buried on 8 October 1888, with the undertaker picking up the expenses himself.

There was one more oddity in this case that contributed to the many conspiracy theories that abounded as people tried to find some pattern in Jack's unordered madness. It was not surprising that Kate would use Kelly as a surname rather than Conway or Eddowes, because she lived with John Kelly. What seemed curious, though, were her choices for first names. When she was at the pawn shop collecting money for Kelly's boots, she gave her name as Jane Kelly. The night of her murder, when she had to give the police her name before she could be released, she called herself Mary Ann Kelly. The real name of Jack's fifth and final victim was Mary Jane Kelly, a coincidence that has fuelled theories for years that the two women knew each other and were both killed because of it.

Chapter 5
Mary Jane Kelly

ary Jane Kelly was singing, which was not unusual for her, but on this night it was irritating one of her neighbours. Catherine Pickett lived near Mary Jane in Miller's Court and had been listening to the singing for 45 minutes. It was 12.30 a.m. on 9 November 1888, and she decided to go downstairs and complain.

Catherine was stopped by her husband. "You leave the poor woman alone," he told her. Mary Jane continued to sing *A Violet from Mother's Grave*:

> *Scenes of my childhood arise before my gaze*
> *Bringing recollections of bygone happy days*

When down in the meadow in childhood I
would roam
No one's left to cheer me now within that good
old home

Mary Jane knew many Irish songs but this was her favourite, and a number of witnesses heard her singing it that night. Mary Ann Cox, a 31-year-old prostitute also living in Miller's Court, saw Kelly with a man at 11.45 p.m. They were heading into Mary Jane's room and Cox noticed she was very drunk. "Good night, Mary Jane," Cox said. "Good night," Mary Jane replied. "I'm going to have a song." It was a cold, wet night and Cox returned to her room once or twice during the next couple of hours to warm up before heading out to find another client. Each time she noticed light still coming from the room and could hear Mary Jane singing:

Only a violet I pluck'd when but a boy
And oft 'time when I'm sad at heart this flow'r has
giv'n me joy

Mary Jane had good reason to be sad over how her life had turned out, although she certainly accepted some of the responsibility for it. More than once she gave a warning to her young friend, Lizzie Albrook, who lived in Miller's Court but worked at a nearby lodging house in Dorset Street. "About the last thing she said to me was 'Whatever you do don't you do wrong and turn out as I did'," Albrook later recalled. "She had often spoken to me in this way and warned me against going on the street as she had done. She told me, too, that she was heartily sick of the life she was leading and wished she had money enough to go back to Ireland where her people lived."

Most of what is known about Mary Jane came from what she told other people, but she was definitely born in Ireland, probably in 1863, making her 25 years old in 1888. Some reports said she was known as Marie Jeanette rather than Mary Jane. Her family moved to Wales when she was very young. She married a coal miner in 1879, but he was killed three years later in a mine explosion. Mary Jane may have had a son from this marriage, but this has never been confirmed. Shortly after her husband's death, she moved in with a cousin in Cardiff and it was there that she was introduced to a life of prostitution. Venereal disease and a year in an infirmary followed. Mary Jane then moved to London in 1884 and became a prostitute in the West End. Literate and better educated than most prostitutes, she stood 5 feet, 7 inches and had an hourglass figure and considerable charm. Her blond hair, blue eyes and fair complexion kept a steady stream of men at her door. Joseph Barnett, her later paramour, said that after her arrival in London she worked in a high-class brothel, frequently rode in a carriage and accompanied one gentleman to France. "She did not remain long [in France]" Joseph Barnett said. "She said she did not like the part, but whether it was the part or purpose I cannot say."

Gradually, between 1884 and 1886, her taste for alcohol grew and Mary Jane's life began to spiral downwards and towards London's East End. For the next year or so, she lived with two different men until, on 8 April 1887, she met Barnett. "We then had a drink together, and I made arrangements to see her on the following day, a Saturday," Barnett told the inquest. "On that day we both of us agreed that we should remain together." Barnett was a labourer and a market porter, licensed to work at a fish market. He did his best to take care of Mary Jane, although they were evicted from one place they lived for being drunk and not paying rent. In February or March 1888, the couple moved to 13 Miller's Court, off Dorset Street.

Dorset Street ran east-west between Commercial and Crispin Streets and was flanked by old, brick-built properties whose doors opened directly onto the street. The street was well known for its poverty and crime. (In 1887, businessman and early sociologist Charles Booth produced a "poverty map" of London, colour-coding different regions according to quality of life and labour measures. Dorset Street was one of the few areas to be black-coded as the "lowest class", which categorised it as "vicious and semi-criminal".)

Occupying either end of the street on the north side were two pubs, the three-storey Britannia at the eastern end and the similarly imposing Horn of Plenty at the western end. Three alleyways ran out of the northern side of Dorset Street, one of them Miller's Court, which contained low-grade housing. The three-foot-wide entrance to Miller's Court was about a quarter of the way along the street from the eastern end, nestled between 26 and 27 Dorset Street, both of which were owned by grocer and slum landlord John McCarthy. He resided at No. 27 and carried on his chandler's business from its ground floor shop. No. 26 he used as a storeroom. At 35 Dorset Street, opposite the entrance to Miller's Court, was Crossingham's lodging house where earlier victim Annie Chapman had lived.

No. 13 Miller's Court was in fact the back parlour of 26 Dorset Street, partitioned off from the rest of the building and having its own entrance off the alleyway. The room was only 12 square feet and had a fireplace, bed, bedside stand, table and chair, and small cupboard containing cheap crockery and empty bottles of ginger beer. Mary Jane took the room under her own name, paying a rent of four shillings and sixpence a week.

Barnett and Mary Jane continued to live in Miller's Court through the summer of 1888, even after Barnett lost his job. Barnett would not allow Mary Jane to work the street and did everything he could to keep her away from it, but she began to drift towards it as money became scarce for the couple. After the "double event", however, Mary Jane's fear rose too. "I bought newspapers, and I read to her everything about the murders, which she asked me about," Barnett later said.

On 1 October 1888, *The Times* wrote: "The fact that another murder had been committed soon became known in the neighbourhood, and long before daybreak the usually quiet thoroughfare was the scene of great excitement."

And the *East London Observer* reported on 6 October 1888: "The appearance of East London early on the Sunday morning as the news of the murders was known – and indeed, all day – almost baffles description. Every window of every inhabited room in the vicinity was thrown open, for the better view of the inmates; and seats at these windows were being openly sold and eagerly bought. On the outskirts of the vast chattering, excited assemblage of humanity, costermongers, who sold everything in the way of edibles, from fish and bread to fruits and sweets, and newspaper vendors whose hoarse cries only added to the confusion of sounds heard on every hand, were doing exceedingly large trades."

The police were also out in full force, guarding both murder sites. As *The Star* noted, "No one could say there were not enough police in the East-end today. The blue helmets were thick as bees in a clover field."

No one made more money than the newspapers, which broadcast constant updates and broadsheets. Local enterprise didn't suffer, either. Just as occurred after Annie Chapman was murdered in Hanbury Street, local residents began charging admission for people wanting to see the very spots where the murders had taken place. Even the International Working Men's Club would only let people look around its premises for a fee. Local fairs provided "entertainments" based on the Ripper and many sold defensive weapons for women.

Overwhelmingly, though, those who lived in the East End had great sympathy for the victims. Hundreds of letters were received by the newspapers, condemning the police, calling for rewards and suggesting solutions to the problems of the East End.

* * *

Social unrest was nothing new in London and Sir Charles Warren, who had become the Metropolitan Police Commissioner in 1886, played a major role in inciting it a year before the Ripper murders. During the summer of 1887, large numbers of the destitute unemployed began campaigning in Trafalgar Square. Warren, fearing these meetings would lead to riots, asked Home Secretary Henry Matthews to ban all meetings in the square. A meeting to challenge the ban was called for on 13 November 1887. More than 100,000 unemployed people and socialist sympathisers – including George Bernard Shaw, writer William Morris, artist Walter Crane and female activist Annie Bryant – swarmed towards Trafalgar Square that day, where they were met by 2000 police who beat them and drove them into the side streets. Those running towards the square were charged down by police horses. Warren himself was mounted on one of them. "Bloody Sunday", as it came to be remembered, was an ugly day that ended with the death of two of the demonstrators. The press and the socialists would never forget the day or the role Sir

Charles Warren played in it.

After the East End murders began, George Bernard Shaw, referring to Bloody Sunday, voiced his views in a letter to *The Star*, printed on 24 September 1888. The letter said in part:

"Will you allow me to make a comment on the success of the Whitechapel murderer in calling attention for a moment to the social question? Less than a year ago the West-end press, headed by ... *The Times* and the *Saturday Review*, were literally clambering for the blood of the people – hounding on Sir Charles Warren to thrash and muzzle the scum who dared to complain they were starving – applauding to the skies the open class bias of those magistrates and judges who zealously did their very worst in the criminal proceedings which followed ... The *Saturday Review* was still frankly for hanging the appellants; and *The Times* denounced them as 'pests of society' ... Now all is changed. Private enterprise has succeeded where Socialism failed. Whilst we conventional Social Democrats were wasting our time on education, agitation, and organisation, some independent genius has taken the matter in hand, and by simply murdering and disembowelling women, converted the proprietary press to an inept sort of communism."

There was total resistance on the part of the Home Office, under the guidance of Henry Matthews, to giving any kind of reward for the capture of the Ripper. Even the murder of Elizabeth Stride did nothing to persuade him otherwise, in spite of the wishes of Warren and many others.

"It is unfortunate," the *Dublin Express* wrote, "that the Home Secretaryship should be in the hands of a Minister without sagacity or sympathy, who looks with cold indifference on the excitement caused by the murders, and doggedly resists all pressure to offer a reward."

The City of London, where Catherine Eddowes had been murdered, however, had no such reluctance and it announced a £500 reward almost immediately after her murder. A number of vigilante committees were set up and began unofficially patrolling the streets at night. Extra policemen also did the rounds, and often these two groups ended up eyeing each other suspiciously after dark. The increased heat from all sides, however, did seem to stop the Ripper. As the days turned into weeks, the murders ceased, even during the London fog that descended in mid-October 1888. Fewer people were out on the streets at night and tradespeople complained that their business was down by half.

Jack the Ripper, however, wasn't finished, merely resting, and he was saving his best for last.

* * *

As October was coming to a close, Joseph Barnett and Mary Jane had a fight, during which she broke one of the windows in their room. The lack of money was wearing them down, but the biggest point of contention was that Mary Jane was allowing a prostitute friend of hers to sleep with them in the room. For Barnett, this was the last straw. "She would never have gone wrong again and I shouldn't have left her if it had not been for prostitutes stopping at the house," Barnett said. "She only let them because she was good hearted and did not like to refuse them shelter on cold bitter nights."

Barnett moved out, but they remained on friendly terms and he came by to see Mary Jane almost every day, giving her money when he could.

One of the prostitutes, Maria Harvey, stayed with Mary Jane on 5 and 6 November before finding her own lodgings. Perhaps being alone after dark frightened Mary Jane, because on the evening of 7 November she purchased a halfpenny candle from McCarthy's shop. The next afternoon, 8 November, she spent with Harvey, who left her just after Barnett arrived for a visit. He, in turn, went back to his boarding house about 8.00 p.m. and Mary Jane reportedly headed for the Ten Bells pub and had a drink with Elizabeth Foster.

(In 1888, a pub stood on almost every corner in the East End. Among the patrons were women soliciting for clients. Because they could be arrested for prostitution if a policeman saw them standing in one location, these women tended to keep moving and would often walk from one pub to another and back again as they looked for business.)

At 11.00 p.m., Mary Jane was seen drunk in the Britannia pub. Sometime during the evening, she also ate a meal of fish and potatoes.

When Mary Ann Cox saw Mary Jane heading into her

room 45 minutes later, she described her friend's companion as "a short, stout man, shabbily dressed. He had on a longish coat, very shabby, and carried a pot of ale in his hand." Cox also told the inquest the man wore a round hard billycock hat and he had a "blotchy face and full carroty moustache." Cox returned home for the last time at 3.00 a.m. and said the light was out in Mary Jane's room and all was quiet.

Elizabeth Prater, who occupied the room above Mary Jane's, came back at 1.00 a.m. Waiting at the entrance to Miller's Court for the man she was living with, Prater saw no one and, after a visit to McCarthy's shop, went to her room alone at 1.20 a.m. Mary Jane was no longer singing. "I should have seen a glimmer of light in going up the stairs if there had been a light in the deceased's room, but I noticed none," she later testified. "The partition was so thin I could have heard Kelly walk about in the room. I went to bed at half-past one and barricaded the door with two tables."

Prater was quite drunk and fell soundly asleep, but was woken up some time between 3.30 and 4.00 a.m. when her kitten, Diddles, walked across her neck. "As I was turning round I heard a suppressed cry of 'Oh – murder!' in a faint voice," Prater said, adding that this was not unusual in that street and she did not take "particular notice" of it before going back to sleep. Her story was backed up by Sarah Lewis, who had gone to visit a friend in Miller's Court at 2.30 a.m. Lewis fell asleep in her friend's chair and was awakened when she heard the clock strike at 3.30 a.m. "I could not sleep," she testified. "I sat awake until nearly four, when I heard a female's voice shouting 'Murder!' loudly. It seemed like the voice of a young woman ... I took no notice as there was only one scream." It is very likely that both women heard Mary Jane Kelly's last cry for help.

Dawn broke on Friday, 9 November 1888, and life around Miller's Court seemed normal. Mary Jane had not paid her rent in some weeks and owed 29 shillings. The landlord, John McCarthy, had reached the end of his patience and sent his assistant, Thomas Bowyer, to No. 13 to ask for some money. Not getting a reply when he knocked, and finding the door locked, he went to the window he knew was broken and pulled aside the curtain. He saw "two pieces of flesh lying on the table" and, looking further, a body on the bed and blood on the floor. "I at once went very quietly to Mr McCarthy." On confirming the discovery, McCarthy was left speechless and then sent Bowyer for the police, following a few minutes later himself after drinking a glass of brandy. Inspector Beck sent for a doctor and, with several officers, returned with McCarthy and Bowyer to wait outside Mary Jane's room. Dr Phillips, thinking police bloodhounds were coming, decided not to enter the room. Finally, at 1.30 p.m., Inspector Thomas Arnold, who headed up the Whitechapel Division of the Metropolitan Police, arrived to say no dogs would be coming and he ordered McCarthy to break down the locked door.

"The sight we saw I cannot drive away from my mind," McCarthy told *The Times*. "It looked more like the work of a devil than of a man. The poor woman's body was lying on the bed, undressed. She had been completely disembowelled, and her entrails has been taken out and placed on the table. It was those that I had seen when I looked through the window and took to be lumps of flesh. The woman's nose had been cut off, and her face gashed beyond recognition. Both her breasts too had been cut clean away and placed by the side of her liver and other entrails on the table. I had heard a great deal about the Whitechapel murders, but I declare to god I had never expected to see such a sight as this. The body was, of course, covered with blood, and so was the bed. The whole scene is more than I can describe. I hope I may never see such a sight again. It is most extraordinary that nothing should have been heard by the neighbours, as there are people passing backwards and forwards at all hours of the night, but no one heard so much as a scream."

Faced with the horror, McCarthy had a few of the details wrong about the location of various body parts. What he didn't have wrong was the absolute savagery inflicted on the young woman.

Mary Jane's body was removed to the mortuary attached to St. Leonard's Church, Shoreditch, and the post-mortem was conducted by Dr Phillips, Dr Thomas Bond and two other physicians. Bond's report was lost until 1987, when it was returned anonymously to Scotland Yard. He had examined Mary Jane's body at the scene before its removal for the post-mortem. He referred to the body as "lying naked" but, in fact, it was clothed in a thin chemise. The fingers of the right hand were clenched and the left arm was close to the body with the forearm lying across what was left of the abdomen. "The whole of the surface of the abdomen & thighs was removed & the abdominal Cavity emptied of its viscera," the report stated. "The breasts were cut off, the arms mutilated by several jagged wounds & the face hacked beyond recognition of the features."

When Barnett went to see the body on 10 November, he identified Mary Jane "by the ear and eyes, which are all that I can recognise, but I am positive it is the same woman I knew".

Pieces of Kelly were scattered around the murder scene. "The uterus & Kidneys with one breast under the head," Bond wrote, "the other breast by the Rt foot, the Liver between the feet, the intestines by the right side & the spleen by the left side of the body. The flaps removed from the abdomen and thighs were on a table."

Missing was Mary Jane's heart.

Inspector Frederick Abberline, on examining the room, also found something else. "There were traces of a large fire having been kept up in the grate, so much so that it had melted the spout of a kettle," Abberline told the inquest, adding he felt the fire had been set in order to give the killer some light with which to do his work. "An impression has gone abroad that the murderer took away the key of the room," he said. "[Joseph] Barnett informs me that it has been missing for some time, and since it has been lost they have put their hand through the broken window, and moved back the catch. It is quite easy." This would explain how the door came to be locked, for the killer would have seen Mary Jane unlock the door in this fashion and would have locked it the same way as he left.

Home Secretary Henry Matthews was still not allowing a reward, but pressure was being brought to bear by the government and a compromise was reached. Although he actually resigned a couple of days before, Sir Charles Warren's name appeared on a document released on Saturday, 10 November:

MURDER – PARDON. – Whereas on November 8 or 9, in Miller Court, Dorset Street, Spitalfields, Mary Janet [sic] Kelly was murdered by some person or persons unknown: the Secretary of State will advise the grant of Her Majesty's gracious pardon to any accomplice, not being a person who contrived or actually committed the murder, who shall give such information and evidence as shall lead to the discovery and conviction of the person or persons who committed the murder.

Queen Victoria had taken an interest in the murders in Whitechapel from the beginning and after the murders of Stride and Eddowes had telephoned the Home Office to express her shock over the situation. In his book *The Complete History of Jack the Ripper,* Philip Sugden quotes a telegram the Queen sent to her Prime Minister, Lord Salisbury, the day after Mary Jane Kelly's murder: "This new most ghastly murder", Her Majesty wrote, "shows the absolute necessity for some very decided action. All these courts must be lit, and our detectives improved. They are not what they should be." Many obviously agreed with the Queen because when Warren's resignation was formally announced in the Commons, it was greeted with cheers from the opposition.

The inquest into the murder was held on Monday, 12 November 1888. Unlike that for the other Ripper victims, it was short. Only seven witnesses appeared and, more significantly, open testimony about what had been done to Kelly's body was very brief because the authorities believed it was important to keep most of the details to themselves. The inquest was over in a few hours, but at 6.00 p.m. that evening, an incident of more significance took place when a man named George Hutchinson walked into the Commercial Street Police Station to give a statement of what he witnessed shortly before the murder.

"On Thursday [8 November 1888] I had been to Romford, and I returned from there about two o'clock on Friday morning, having walked all the way," Hutchinson later told a reporter. "As I passed Thrawl Street I passed a man standing at the corner of the street, and as I went towards Flower and Dean Street, I met the woman Kelly, whom I knew very well, having been in her company a number of times."

"Mr. Hutchinson, will you lend me a sixpence?" Mary Jane asked.

"I cannot, as I am spent out, going down to Romford," he told her.

"Good morning," Mary Jane responded. "I must go and look for some money."

She walked on towards Thrawl Street, where the man Hutchinson had previously seen standing there "came towards her, put his hand on her shoulder, and said something to her which I did not hear; they both burst out laughing. He put his hand again on her shoulder and they both walked slowly towards me." As they passed Hutchinson, "I put down my head to look him in the face, and he turned and looked at me very sternly." The man was about 5 foot, 6 inches tall and 34 or 35 years of age, with a dark complexion and dark moustache turned up at both ends. He "looked like a foreigner". The man aroused suspicion in Hutchinson because he was so well dressed for the East End. "The man I saw carried a small parcel in his hand about 8 inches long and it had a strap round it," he continued. "He had it tightly grasped in his left hand. It looked as though it was covered with dark American cloth. He carried in his right hand, which he laid upon the woman's shoulder, a pair of brown kid gloves. He walked very softly." Hutchinson followed them to Dorset Street and the entrance to Miller's Court. Mary Jane and the man stood there for a couple of minutes and then went up Miller's Court. "I went to look up the court to see if I could see them, but could not," he said. "I stood there for three-quarters of an hour to see if they came down again, but they did not, and so I went away." It was then 3.00 a.m.

His story was corroborated by Sarah Lewis, who was on her way to her friend's place at 2.30 a.m. "When I went into the court, opposite the lodging-house I saw a man with a wideawake [wary, knowing look]," Lewis testified at the inquest. "There was no one talking to him. He was a stout-looking man, and not very tall. The hat was black. I did not take any notice of his clothes. The man was looking up the court; he seemed to be waiting or looking for someone." She had obviously seen Hutchinson. For his part, Hutchinson was convinced he would recognise the man anywhere and spent considerable time in the following few days walking all over the neighbourhood looking for the man who was most likely Mary Jane's killer.

As much excitement as her death sparked in Whitechapel and elsewhere, no member of Mary Jane's family could be found to take on the expense of her funeral and Joseph Barnett did not have the money to pay for it himself. The sexton attached to Shoreditch Church, H. Wilton, incurred the total cost of the funeral himself. Wilton had been a sexton for over 50 years and "he provided the funeral as a mark of sincere sympathy with the poor people of the neighbourhood, in whose welfare he is deeply interested", the *East London Advertiser* reported. The polished elm and oak coffin was carried in an open car drawn by two horses and taken to the Roman Catholic cemetery at Leystone for interment, "amidst a scene of turbulent excitement.

"The bell of St. Leonard's began tolling at noon, and the signal appeared to draw all the residents in the neighbourhood together. There was an enormous preponderance of women in the crowd," the paper noted. "As the coffin appeared, borne on the shoulders of four men, at the principal gate of the church, the crowd appeared greatly affected. Round the open car in which it was to be placed, men and women struggled desperately to get to touch the coffin. Women with faces streaming with tears cried out, 'God, forgive her!' and every man's head was bared in token of sympathy. The sight was quite remarkable, and the emotion natural and unconstrained."

In life, very few people knew Mary Jane Kelly, but in her death she attained an immortality saved for few because she would always be known as the last victim of Jack the Ripper.

Epilogue

The East End in 1888 was not the London of Big Ben, Buckingham Palace, the Tower of London, or Madame Tussaud's (although more than 100 years later, the famous wax museum featured victim Catherine Eddowes in a grisly exhibit before and after her encounter with Jack). This was the London of horribly overcrowded slums, where the populace lived in the worst conditions imaginable. Filth, poverty and danger predominated, and struggling to survive was a full-time occupation.

"Some years ago, it was fashionable to 'slum' – to walk gingerly about in dirty streets, with great heroism, and go back West again, with a firm conviction that 'something must be done'," Arthur Morrison wrote in the *Palace Journal* on 24 April 1889. "And something must. Children must not be left in these unscoured corners. Their fathers and mothers are hopeless, and must not be allowed to rear a numerous and equally hopeless race. Light the streets better, certainly; but what use in building better houses for these poor creatures to render as foul as those that stand? The inmates may ruin the character of a house, but no house can alter the character of its inmates."

His was not an unusual stance and Morrison hinted at an opinion that would be voiced elsewhere: namely, that the residents of the East End were somehow responsible for their own fate and that those in the rest of London were not in danger.

"So far as the recent diabolical murders are concerned, we would remind our readers that in each instance they have been committed under circumstances which do not imply danger to the respectable classes," the *East London Observer* stated on 6 October 1888. "The murderer has found his victims in the middle of the night, and has induced them to accompany him to corners where none but the depraved would resort. The wretched victims to the seeming mania are selected with marvellous definiteness from the lowest class of prostitutes; and these should now be so well on their guard that further attempts on the part of the murderer should result in his capture. At all events, we hope that all who read our columns will agree with us that the ordinary members of society are not in any danger, and that the thoroughfares of Whitechapel are as safe for the general public as ever."

Of course, the general public rarely ventured into the East End!

Jack the Ripper was able to penetrate the complacency of the rest of London and of the world. His exploits were covered extensively in newspapers as far afield as the United States, Canada and Australia. No one will ever really know conclusively how many women Jack murdered, but Ripperologists have generally settled on the women described in the previous chapters as the five accepted victims. Not all are in agreement, though, some making estimates that range from three to eight victims. Other women were murdered in the year or two surrounding these five murders and all are typically referred to as the Whitechapel murders. Of the other women murdered, the three most often thought to be possible Ripper murders are Martha Tabram, Alice Mackenzie and Frances Coles.

It was two and a half years after Mary Jane Kelly's murder that Police Constable Ernest Thompson was walking his beat and came across the body of Frances Coles. Only on the force for two months, Thompson was on his first night of being alone. In the early hours of 13 February 1891, he approached Swallow Gardens, which was actually a railway arch running from Royal Mint Street to Chambers Street and hadn't seen a flower in years. A man came running out towards him, but as soon as he saw the policeman he turned and ran off in the opposite direction. Thompson went into Swallow Gardens, shone his light into its darkest areas and found the body of a woman with blood flowing from her throat. His first instinct was to pursue the probable killer he had just briefly seen, but then he saw the victim open and close an eye. Because the woman was still alive, police procedure dictated he remain with her. His inability to chase the man he thought was Jack the Ripper would haunt him for the rest of his life.

Frances's throat had been cut with three strikes of a knife, back and forth. A fireman on board a ship, Thomas Sadler, knew her and they had been seen together that evening. He was arrested and charged with her murder, but a thorough inquest cleared him and her killer was never found. Robbery was ruled out as a motive, because her earnings for the night – she was a known prostitute – were found nearby.

Alice Mackenzie's murder was closer in time to the accepted Ripper murders. She was approximately 40 years old, with a love of alcohol and smoking (preferring a pipe to cigarettes). This habit gave her the nickname "Clay Pipe", because she always carried one. Police Constable Walter Andrews entered Castle Alley, just off Whitechapel Road, at 12.50 a.m. on 17 July 1889. It had only been 27 minutes since he had last patrolled the area and found it quiet. This time he saw a woman lying on the pavement, only two feet from a lamp post. Her clothes were pulled up "almost level to the chin", Andrews said. "Her legs and body were exposed. I noticed that blood was running from the left side of the neck."

Opinions about whether Jack the Ripper was the murderer differed considerably. Dr George Bagster Phillips, responsible for the post-mortem, said there was some evidence it could be the same killer, but he personally felt from his own examination that it was not. Dr Thomas Bond, who had written the post-mortem report on Mary Jane Kelly, disagreed. "I see in this murder evidence of similar design to the former Whitechapel murders," he reportedly told Robert Anderson, Assistant Commissioner of Police and head of the Criminal Investigation Department. In his book, *The Lighter Side of My Official Life* (published in 1910), Anderson wrote:

"I am here assuming that the murder of Alice M'Kenzie [sic] on the 17th of July, 1889, was by another hand [than Jack the Ripper]. I was absent from London when it occurred, but the Chief Commissioner investigated the case on the spot and decided that it was an ordinary murder, and not the work of a sexual maniac."

Of all the Whitechapel murders not included in the five accepted murders, the one most likely to have been committed by the Ripper was that of Martha Tabram. Born in 1849, Martha married Henry Tabram in 1869. Two sons and six years later, Henry left her because of her drinking. He gave her an allowance but eventually stopped when he discovered she was living with another man, Henry Turner. By July 1888, Turner had also left Martha.

On Monday, 6 August 1888, Martha and another prostitute met up with two soldiers and were seen with them throughout that evening in various pubs. At 4.45 a.m. the next morning, as John Reeves left his lodgings in the George Yard Buildings, he saw a body on the first-floor landing of the stairwell, lying in a pool of blood. It was Martha, her clothes hiked up, exposing her abdominal area. He ran to find a policeman. Dr Timothy Killeen, who conducted the post-mortem, found 39 stab wounds to her heart, lungs, liver, spleen and stomach. Phillip Sugden, in *The Complete History of Jack the Ripper*, states that both Frederick Abberline, head of the Whitechapel Division of the Metropolitan Police, and Robert Anderson, head of the Criminal Investigation

Department, believed Martha Tabram to be the first Ripper victim – something that other Ripperologists have dismissed in recent years.

The five women killed by Jack's hand were not his only victims. Many other lives were also destroyed by his violence. *The Star* reported one such case on 18 September 1888: "A young butcher named Hennell cut his throat from ear to ear in his parents' house, 76, Enfield-buildings, Ashford-street, Hoxton, last night. The young man was evidently insane. He had repeatedly expressed the fear that they 'were after him for the Whitechapel murder'. His parents had watched him closely for the last few days, and he took the opportunity of his mother leaving the room a minute to cut his throat."

Three weeks later, on Saturday, 13 October 1888, the *Eastern Post & City Chronicle* reported, "The particulars of a case of suicide, which took place at No. 65, Hanbury Street, Spitalfields, a house a few doors away from the spot where the unfortunate woman Annie Chapman was murdered, reached Dr Macdonald, the coroner for North-East Middlesex on Thursday. It appears that the top floor of the address is occupied by a silk weaver named Sodeaux, his wife, and child aged eight years. For some time past Mrs. Sodeaux has been depressed, and since the perpetration of the horrible murders which have taken place in the district she has been greatly agitated. On Sunday she was found to have a razor in her possession, and it was taken from her, as it was thought she meditated suicide. The following day she appeared to be more cheerful, and was left alone with her child. On Wednesday her daughter found her hanging with a rope round her neck to the stair banisters."

* * *

Who was Jack the Ripper? Was he as clever and bold as was thought at the time? Or was he merely lucky? Probably, he was all three.

Although there was no sign of intercourse, he nevertheless fits the profile of a sexual serial killer – a term not even coined then. It is common for modern serial killers to take trophies from their victims. Jack's trophies seemed to be his victims' organs. Did he really have some anatomical knowledge? Most investigators felt his knowledge of the human anatomy could have been acquired by slaughtermen and butchers as easily as by doctors or medical students. However, the belief that Jack the Ripper might have been a doctor was supported by the close proximity of London Hospital in Whitechapel Road.

Many letters and postcards were written to newspapers and police officials during this time, purportedly from Jack the Ripper, but very few were given any credence. The ones most talked about were the ones signed "Jack the Ripper", but the police eventually felt they knew the real source of those. In a letter to journalist G.R. Sims, dated 23 September 1913, Chief Inspector John George Littlechild wrote, "With regard to the term 'Jack the Ripper' it was generally believed at the Yard that Tom Bullen of the Central News was the originator, but it is probable Moore, who was his chief, was the inventor. It was a smart piece of journalistic work." A great deal of money was made by the newspapers over the months the murders took place, so continuing to captivate the public's attention was in the papers' own interest.

By the time of the Mary Jane Kelly murder in November 1888, most of the doctors involved in the cases believed the killer to be medically insane. Opinions as to the origins and symptoms of this insanity were in huge supply. The October 1888 issue of the *Fortnightly Review*, for example, included an article on "homicidal mania" by a Dr Savage, who shed some insight into the criminal's brain.

"Professor Benedikt of Vienna, it appears, has been for some time making an exhaustive comparison of the brains of criminals, and has devoted especial attention to the cerebral development of murderers," Dr Savage wrote. "He has weighed, measured, and done everything but taste the brains of scores of malefactors. The result of his experience is that he has demonstrated satisfactorily that the brain of a murderer frequently resembles that of a lower animal 'in certain definite ways'. It is fair to suppose that thieving and a monkey like convolution of brain go together ... According to Professor Benedikt murderers brains have a special likeness to those of bears."

(This article prompted the following response from

the *East London Advertiser* on 6 October 1888: "A man with a bear-shaped brain should therefore be avoided – unfortunately there is considerable difficulty in telling the shape of your friend's brain while he is alive.")

While Jack was never captured, there was no lack of suspects for the murders. As with most celebrated murder cases, false confessions happened on a daily basis, usually by men who were very drunk, but all leads were followed by the police. Among the strangest and most colourful suspects to come to light through the years are the following:

Charles Lutwidge Dodgson (aka Lewis Carroll): Born in 1832, Dodgson, despite his religious background, did not take up the priesthood, choosing instead to become a photographer in 1856. In the same year, a new dean, Henry Liddell, arrived at the church, bringing with him a young wife and children, including a daughter called Alice. Dodgson often took Alice and her two sisters out for picnics. On one outing, in 1862, Dodgson invented the outline of the story that eventually became his first "Alice" book. He was begged by Alice Liddell to write the story down and he finally did. *Alice's Adventures in Wonderland* was published in 1865, under the pen-name Dodgson had first used some nine years earlier, Lewis Carroll. In 1996, Richard Wallace published *Jack the Ripper, Light-Hearted Friend*, a book in which he speculated that Carroll and a friend committed the murders. His evidence was supposed anagrams he found in Carroll's work, which Wallace claimed were confessions of the crime.

Epilogue

Prince Albert Victor Christian Edward (known as Eddy): Born in 1864, Queen Victoria's grandson somehow became involved in three different Ripper theories, although he was never a suspect at the time of the murders. The most famous theory is the Royal Family Conspiracy, which first appeared in the BBC programme *Jack the Ripper* in 1973. Eddy was supposedly introduced to a poor Catholic girl named Annie Crook, who worked in a shop on Cleveland Street. They fell in love, secretly married and had a little girl named Alice. Queen Victoria found out and was not amused. Not only was Annie a commoner, but a Catholic as well. Queen Victoria handed the matter over to her prime minister, Lord Salisbury, who in turn gave the task of solving the situation to the Royal physician, William Gull. The story goes that Gull sent men to raid the love nest and take Annie off to one of Gull's hospitals, where she was experimented on until she lost her sanity. During the raid, however, little Alice escaped unharmed with her nanny, Mary Jane Kelly. Kelly, the story continues, told her friends Polly Nichols, Annie Chapman and Lizzie Stride what had happened and they decided to blackmail the government. Gull was again called upon and this time all the women were murdered. Kate Eddowes was not an intended victim, but because she sometimes went by the name of Mary Kelly, her death was a case of mistaken identity.

There was never any actual evidence for this theory, except for the word of Joseph Sickert whose father, Walter, just happened to be another suspect in the murders. The

Royal Conspiracy doesn't end there. The little girl, Alice, it was said, actually grew up to marry Walter Sickert, the painter, and was the mother of Joseph.

Walter Sickert: The most sensational book in recent years on the Ripper murders is *Portrait of a Killer: Jack the Ripper – Case Closed*, written by Patricia Cornwell (2003). Cornwell makes the case for artist Walter Sickert (an associate of James McNeill Whistler) being the Ripper, showing forensically a link between him and some of the many letters sent to the newspapers and the police. While Sickert may well have written some of the hoax letters, the rest of Cornwell's proof of his guilt is based on what she perceives in many of his paintings. A number of Ripperologists, however, have shown that Sickert was likely not even in England at the time some of the murders were committed.

Montague John Druitt: Druitt is believed to be the number one suspect by many people, including Melville Macnaghten, who became Assistant Chief Constable in 1889. In response to an article in *The Sun*, Macnaghten wrote what is now considered to be one of the most important documents on the Jack the Ripper case.

"(1) A Mr M. J. Druitt, said to be a doctor & of good family – who disappeared at the time of the Miller's Court murder, & whose body (which was said to have been upwards of a month in the water) was found in the Thames on 31st December – or about 7 weeks after that murder," Macnaghten said. "He was sexually insane and from private information I have little doubt but that his own family believed him to have been the murderer."

Mental illness ran in Druitt's family and he feared ending up like his mother, who was committed six months before his suicide. Again, there is little in the way of evidence to tie him to the murders.

A website devoted to a thorough examination of all aspects of the murders – Casebook: Jack the Ripper (www.casebook.org) – lists suspects according to popularity among their readership. Of the more than 62,000 votes cast on the site, the top four suspects are James Maybrick, Joseph Barnet, Francis Tumblety, and George Chapman.

James Maybrick: Maybrick was never really a suspect until the "Maybrick Diaries" surfaced in the early 1990s, supposedly written by him and containing a confession to the crimes. Despite the fact that the person who "found" these diaries has since admitted more than once that he and his wife forged them, many people still continue to believe Maybrick is a prime suspect. He was a frequent user of arsenic, which made him paranoid and delusional. Eventually, he himself was murdered by poisoning and his wife, Florence, was charged and convicted of the murder. Not long before her execution date, her sentence was reduced and she served 15 years before being released.

Joseph Barnett: The lover of Mary Jane Kelly was interviewed by the police for four hours about her murder and they seemed satisfied with his alibi, but he has never been ruled out as a suspect. The theory is he killed the other prostitutes to scare Mary Jane into leaving prostitution and when he realised that wasn't going to happen, he killed her as well.

The last two men, George Chapman and Francis Tumblety, seem to be the two most likely killers of all the known suspects. The problem with both of them is their respective age at the times of the killings. Most witnesses had put the killer in the 28- to 40-year age range. That would make Chapman too young at the time of the Ripper murders and Tumblety too old. However, eyewitness accounts can be mistaken, especially in the dark, so both men still are believed by many to be the most likely candidates for Jack the Ripper.

George Chapman (born Sevrin Klosowski): Born in Poland in 1865, Sevrin Klosowski studied to become a surgeon from 1880 to 1885. Best estimates are that he arrived in England in February or March 1887. He worked as a hairdresser's assistant and then ran his own barber shop at 126 Cable Street, St. George's in the East. It is likely he lived there during the Ripper murders. In October 1889, he married Lucy Baderski in a Roman Catholic ceremony. He was, however, already married to someone in Poland. She came to London on hearing of his new marriage, but finally gave up and went home after the birth of Klosowski and Baderski's son. After the death of the child in 1891, the couple moved to New Jersey in the United States, where he set up a barber shop. He quarrelled with Lucy constantly and once tried to kill her.

Epilogue

According to a story in the *Daily Chronicle* of 23 March 1903, "he held her down on the bed, and pressed his face against her mouth to keep her from screaming. At that moment a customer entered the shop immediately in front of the room, and Koslowski got up to attend him. The woman chanced to see a handle protruding from underneath the pillow. She found, to her horror, that it was a sharp and formidable knife, which she promptly hid." He later told her he had intended to cut her head off. Pregnant and scared, she fled to London.

Klosowski soon followed and, in the winter of 1893, he met a woman named Annie Chapman – coincidentally the same name as one of the murder victims. They lived together for a year before he began to cheat and the pregnant Annie left. He took her surname, however, and from then on was known as George Chapman. Between then and 22 October 1902, he entered into three phoney marriages, beat all three women violently and then poisoned them to death. His luck finally ran out with Maud Marsh, when a doctor would not sign the death certificate. The bodies of his two previous "wives" were exhumed and he was charged with three counts of murder. Convicted of the Marsh murder, he was executed on 7 April 1903. From the moment of Chapman's arrest, there was one man who fervently believed that at last Jack the Ripper was behind bars. That man was Frederick Abberline, former Chief Detective Inspector of Scotland Yard. The *Pall Mall Gazette* reported Abberline saying:

"I have been so struck with the remarkable coincidences

in the two series of murders that I have not been able to think of anything else for several days past – not, in fact, since the Attorney-General made his opening statement at the recent trial, and traced the antecedents of Chapman before he came to this country in 1888. Since then the idea has taken full possession of me, and everything fits in and dovetails so well that I cannot help feeling that this is the man we struggled so hard to capture fifteen years ago. My interest in the Ripper cases was especially deep. I had for fourteen years previously been an inspector of Police in Whitechapel, but when the murders began I was at the Central Office at Scotland Yard. On the application of Superintendent Arnold I went back to the East End just before Annie Chapman was found mutilated, and as chief of the detective corps I gave myself up to the study of the cases. Many a time ... instead of going home when I was off duty, I used to patrol the district until four or five o'clock in the morning, and, while keeping my eyes wide open for clues of any kind, have many and many a time given those wretched, homeless women, who were Jack the Ripper's special prey, fourpence or sixpence for a shelter to get them away from the streets and out of harm's way."

Abberline continued, "There are a score of things which make one believe that Chapman is the man, and you must understand that we have never believed all those stories about Jack the Ripper being dead, or that he was a lunatic, or anything of that kind. For instance, the date of the arrival in England coincides with the beginning of the series of murders in Whitechapel; there is a coincidence also in the fact that the murders ceased in London when 'Chapman' went to America, while similar murders began to be perpetrated in America after he landed there. The fact that he studied medicine and surgery in Russia before he came here is well established, and it is curious to note that the first series of murders was the work of an expert surgeon, while the recent poisoning cases were proved to be done by a man with more than an elementary knowledge of medicine. The story told by 'Chapman's' wife of the attempt to murder her with a long knife while in America is not to be ignored."

Abberline saw no conflict with a person switching modes of murder.

"A man who could watch his wives being slowly tortured to death by poison, as he did, was capable of anything; and the fact that he should have attempted, in such a cold-blooded manner to murder his first wife with a knife in New Jersey, makes one more inclined to believe in the theory that he was mixed up in the two series of crimes."

Francis Tumblety: Tumblety was born in either Ireland or Canada, about 1833. By the time he started working in a chemist's as a teenager, Tumblety and his family had moved to Rochester, New York. By 1850 he had started his own very lucrative practice as an Indian herb doctor and a long career of moving from one country to another, often one step ahead of the police. Tumblety was arrested in Montreal, Canada, in 1857 for attempting to abort the pregnancy of a local prostitute with pills and one of his potions. A week later he was released and no trial took place. Within the next year or two he moved to Saint John, New Brunswick, and reportedly presented quite the figure around town.

"The doctor cut a great dash here. He purported to be an eclectic physician; he lodged at a leading hotel, and he acquired a large practice," *The Daily Sun* of Saint John reported on 22 November 1888. "Loudly dressed, mounted on a white horse and followed by one or more hounds, he made quite a sensation when going through the streets on his way to his patients. He was considered a quack by many, but that did not prevent him from doing a good business."

Again he ran afoul of the law when a patient, James Portmore, died while taking medicine prescribed by Tumblety. He tried to deflect suspicion from himself at the inquest. When that didn't work, he crossed into the United States and relocated to Calais, Maine, subsequently moving from there to Boston.

In an article about Tumblety in the *Rochester Democrat and Republican*, dated 3 December 1888, it was reported that he met well-known lawyer Colonel C.A. Dunham in Boston. Durham, said the article, recalled being a guest at a dinner one evening at Tumblety's. He asked his host why no women were present.

"'No, Colonel, I don't know any such cattle, and if I did I would, as your friend, sooner give you a dose of quick poison than take you into such danger'," Tumblety replied before the men assembled at the table. According to Durham, "[Tumblety] then broke into a homily on the sin and folly of dissipation [and] fiercely denounced all woman and especially fallen women. Then he invited us into his office where he illustrated his lecture, so to speak. One side of this room was entirely occupied with cases, outwardly resembling wardrobes. When the doors were opened quite a museum was revealed – tiers of shelves with glass jars and cases, some round and others square, filled with all sorts of antomical [sic] specimens. The 'doctor' placed on a table a dozen or more jars containing, as he said, the matrices [wombs] of every class of women. Nearly a half of one of these cases was occupied exclusively with these specimens."

Tumblety left the United States for London in the late 1860s and wound up in Liverpool in 1874. He spent the next several years travelling back and forth between England and the United States, showing up again in Liverpool in June 1888. There he was arrested on 7 November on charges of gross indecency (the Victorian euphemism for homosexual activities). More significantly, he was charged on 12 November on suspicion of the Whitechapel murders, which suggests he was not in jail on 9 November when Mary Jane Kelly was murdered. He posted bail on 16 November, slipped under police surveillance and fled to France under the alias of Frank Townsend on 24 November. From there he took the steamer *La Bretagne* to New York City.

New York City's Chief Inspector Byrnes soon discovered

where Tumblety was living and kept him under surveillance. However, Tumblety could not be arrested because the crime for which he was under bond was not extraditable.

While the newspapers in the United States covered his exploits extensively, little was written about him in the British press. Scotland Yard may have been embarrassed over letting a top suspect slip through their fingers so easily. Detective Chief Inspector John Littlechild, the ex-head of the Special Branch at Scotland Yard, felt in 1888 that "amongst the suspects" Tumblety was "to my mind a very likely one". He even confided his suspicions much later to journalist G.R. Sims in a letter dated 23 September 1913 (a letter that was only rediscovered by a Ripper researcher in 1993). Ripper or not, the murders seemed to cease once Tumblety left the country.

In their article on Tumblety, the *Rochester Democrat and Republican* reported some observations of Mr. Edward Haywood, of the Bureau of Accounts in the State Department, who had known Tumblety since boyhood. "When it was first mentioned in the newspapers that there were suspicions connecting Tumblety with the Whitechapel murders, Mr. Haywood immediately said that the theory was quite tenable," the paper stated.

"Knowing him as I do I should not be the least surprised if he turned out to be Jack the Ripper," Haywood told the paper.

Tumblety died in the United States in 1903. Reportedly found among his belongings were copper rings similar to the

Epilogue

ones missing from Annie Chapman's fingers at the time of her murder.

Even with new documents still surfacing, it is highly unlikely that we will ever know for sure the identity of Jack the Ripper. His legend has grown in the century or so since the crimes were committed. Books are still written, movies made, theories expounded upon and other murders executed in his memory. However, there was nothing romantic about Jack. He was a brutal, cold-blooded serial killer who chose as his victims a group of poor women who were struggling to survive in an environment that never gave them a chance. He not only took their lives, but humiliated their bodies after death. If anyone should be remembered, it is them.

Bibliography

Begg, Paul. *The Jack the Ripper A to Z*. London, UK: Headline, 1994.

Cornwell, Patricia. *Portrait of a Killer: Jack the Ripper – Case Closed*. New York, USA: Berkley Publishing Group, 2003.

Rumbelow, Donald. *The Complete Jack the Ripper*. London, UK: Penguin Books, 1988.

Ryder, Stephen P. (ed.). *Casebook: Jack the Ripper*. www.casebook.org.

Sugden, Philip. *The Complete History of Jack the Ripper*. New York, USA: Carroll & Graf, 1994.

Acknowledgements

I am always grateful to the writers who came before me, leaving a trail of history to follow in news clippings, magazine articles and books.

Special thanks to:

- My friend Seema Shah, who listened patiently to my tales of Jack and his victims.
- Aaron Chapman of the band The Town Pants for allowing me to quote from "Dark Annie", the song he wrote about his ancestor Annie Chapman, one of Jack's victims. The song is included in the band's CD *Piston Baroque*.
- Altitude Publishing for being so supportive and allowing me to indulge my love of history.
- My editor, Georgina Montgomery, who made the editing process less painful and my book more readable than it would have been without her.

My gratitude also to all the cats in my life who have supported both me and my writing – you know who you are.

About the Author

Susan McNicoll lives in Vancouver, British Columbia, Canada, where she divides her time between writing and running her own bookkeeping and tax accounting business. Susan's life-long love of words and history has been the main focus of her writing career, which began in the 1970s when she worked as a reporter for *The Ottawa Journal*. Her book on post-war Canadian theatre history, *Everyman Had Its Day*, is scheduled for publication in 2005 by Ronsdale Press. In this, her third, *Amazing Stories* book, she crosses the ocean to tackle that most famous of serial killers, Jack the Ripper. In doing so, Susan returns to a country where she spent many of her formative years, including three at Tortington Park School in Sussex. Although her published work to date has been in non-fiction, Susan is currently working on a series of fables based on the four seasons of healing.